Bedfordshire's Yesteryears

The Family
Childhood & Schooldays

Brenda Fraser-Newstead

First published November 1993
by
The Book Castle
12 Church Street
Dunstable
Bedfordshire LU5 4RU

© Brenda Fraser-Newstead, 1993.

ISBN 1 871199 96 4

Computer typeset by Keyword, Aldbury, Hertfordshire.
Printed in Great Britain by the Alden Press, Oxford.

The 'Bedfordshire's Yesteryears' oral history series is planned to comprise:
volume 1 : The Family, Childhood and Schooldays
volume 2 : The Rural Scene
volume 3 : Craftsmen and Trades People
volume 4 : War Times and Civil Matters

Front Cover: Pretty as a picture! A child in white lace, cottons and petticoats (circa 1900). Little boys were often similarly dressed, with long flowing curls. At the age of about four years, the boys would be 'breeched', when their locks would be cut, and trousers took the place of petticoats.
Photo: courtesy of Frank Newstead.

CONTENTS

FOREWORD

It gives me great pleasure in this, the European Year of Elderly People and Solidarity between Generations, to prepare a foreword for Brenda Fraser-Newstead's book. It is very generous of her to wish to support research into Alzheimer's disease, one of the most awful conditions to afflict mankind, especially the elderly. Alzheimer's disease is the commonest cause of dementia and increasing confusion in older people, and also sadly some of the younger. It results from the destruction of brain cells and the effect this has upon the biochemistry of the brain.

Approximately one person in fifty aged sixty-five to seventy, rising to one person in five by the age of eighty and over has a dementing illness, and the majority of these people suffer with Alzheimer's disease. This leads to a loss of memory but more importantly an inability to think properly, to use language, to carry out simple day-to-day tasks, to control bowels and bladder, and to give and return love. The behavioural problems that result can destroy the life of those who care for the sufferer, as well as that of the sufferer him or herself. For every person suffering with Alzheimer's disease there are usually two or three others whose lives are affected, and these are often elderly people trying to cope with their own physical infirmities as well as the relentless progression of this disorder in a person whom they hold dear.

I would urge those of you reading these words to purchase this book, not only because of its interest and contents but also to help support the research that we have to undertake to try and conquer this awful affliction.

G K Wilcock BSc, DM(Oxon), FRCP
Professor in Care of the Elderly,
University of Bristol and
Honorary Consultant Physician,
Frenchay Healthcare NHS Trust

To my mother, Alice May,
source of my inspiration

INTRODUCTION

One of our most important sources of tangible history is our longest-surviving local residents. Here the reader is introduced to social history through first-hand experience. During a period of very radical social reform and technical innovation, many people, including those portrayed in this book, have experienced a continual process of change such as many of us will never encounter. Born at around the turn of the century, these individuals have seen two World Wars and have witnessed other amazing changes such as the advent of radio, television, telephone and communications; decimalisation and the emergence of the computerised society; motorised travel with motorways and personalised transportation; air travel, package holidays and space exploration; supermarkets, convenience foods and mass consumerism; property ownership, geographical mobility and the change from an extended family unit to the nuclear family; the film industry and the pop industry; hedonism and the diminution of religious influence; the emancipation of women and the youth culture. The generation of people about whom I have written are indeed amazing, if only for their ability to adapt and to survive. How much we could learn from these people if we only gave them the opportunity to inform us!

During my lifetime I have developed an affinity with the past and an insatiable appetite for knowledge of local history, combined with a reverence for the rural lifestyle. In researching my book I have been privileged to be able, through my contacts, to enjoy the delights of an earlier age. I am grateful for this personal glimpse into family and community life, in having been enabled, as it were, to reach out and touch the past. I am fortunate in having been given a guided tour of recent local history by the very people who wrote it.

Brenda Fraser-Newstead

The Author's family. Frances Mabel Slough (grandmother) seated left, with daughter Alice May (mother) far left, and sons John 'Jac' Alfred, standing, and Arthur Frederick in foreground.

Elizabeth Slough (Frances Slough's sister-in-law) seated right, with children Kit on left, Ron (babe), Lillian, Jack and Bob. Circa 1911.

About the Author

Brenda Fraser-Newstead spent many years in the world of commerce and has been a teacher, author and examiner of Business Studies, and a company director. In recent years, however, she has forsaken that involvement and found rewarding work in social welfare and the teaching of children with special needs. She originates from Wheathampstead in Hertfordshire, but her father was a Lutonian and she herself has lived in Bedfordshire for some twenty-five years.

Acknowledgements

The author wishes to thank, in particular, the contributors to this project, without whose help the book would not have materialised. Thanks also to the very many people, too numerous to mention personally, who have kindly given advice, assistance and support. The author's daughter, Yasmina, deserves credit for her valuable assistance in editing and proof-reading. Also, the author's husband, Bryan, for painstaking reproduction of a wonderful selection of photographs, deserves a special mention. Unless otherwise credited, photographs have been taken from the individual contributors' private collections. Gratitude also to the following:

Professor C K Wilcock
Mrs Vivienne Evans
Mr Eric Sabey
Revd. David Lewthwaite and
    Maulden Historical Society
The Bedfordshire Times
Mrs B Chambers,
    The Bedfordshire Magazine
The County Records Office
Mr & Mrs W Juffs, Wootton
The Shuttleworth Collection
The Luton News
The Dunstable Gazette

Bedfordshire Social Services
The Imperial War Museum
Mrs H S Brown,
    Moggerhanger
Mr & Mrs W R Parrott,
    Milton Ernest
Mr E Baldock, Dunstable
Mr A Woodward, Keysoe
The European Design
    Consortium, Cranfield
Staff at the Goldington Social
    Centre, Barkers Lane,
    Bedford

THE FAMILY

THE FAMILY

Introduction

Each member of the Victorian and Edwardian family knew his or her place, and children were brought up to respect their mother and father, and in fact, adults in general ('elders and betters'). Most families were patriarchal, since the husband and father was the provider and therefore the head of the family. 'You'd better ask you father' was a common response to childish pleas.

In large families, as most were, the children played their part and did their allocated household duties. Even after the introduction of compulsory schooling, some children were clearly kept away from school by parents in order to work in various ways, to boost the family's income. A child could be gainfully employed potato or stone picking, acorn or manure gathering, for instance. Girls were occasionally allowed time off to help a sick mother.

The elderly were regarded with respect, as, in such closed societies as tended to exist in rural areas, knowledge gained through years of experience would be handed down from generation to generation. Therefore old age carried far more status than it does in today's society with its technologies and media influences.

Housewives of the period were energetic providers. With no gas or electricity supplies, no internal toilet and bathroom facilities, and no internal water supply, household and family management could be an exacting task. Little wonder housewives rarely worked outside the home! Food could be stored in a cool pantry, but obviously deterioration was more rapid without refrigeration. Meat could be salted as a means of preservation, but generally food would be cooked from fresh meat and vegetables and consumed immediately. And one can imagine the size of each meal in families of ten or more members, which was not uncommon.

Food preparation would be carried out on a bleached and scrubbed kitchen table, and cooked on the 'range', heated by fire. Imagine rising early on a dark and bleak wintery morning in an unheated bedroom, washing form a china wash-set in cold water, and then tackling the problem of cleaning the previous day's ashes from the stove and rekindling the fire on which to cook breakfast. If successful, the fire would be aglow and the room warm before the family emerged for breakfast. In some poor families, living in cramped conditions in small 'two up, two down' cottages, children sat on the stairs to eat, with plates balanced precariously on knees!

Chris Creamer at the age of eighty-nine, still tending his kitchen range in Milton Bryan.

Despite living in crowded cottages, it was not uncommon for families to use only one room – the kitchen – and to keep the front parlour 'for best' which meant that it remained unused and unheated except if visitors came, or for use on Sundays, the Sabbath and day of rest, observed by all in the best Christian tradition.

Since the Sabbath was observed conscientiously, anyone working would be subjected to harsh criticism and reprimand. Children were often prevented from playing, made to attend church or chapel and Sunday School. Everyone dressed in their best for Sunday, and roast lunch, the only quality meal of the week, would be cooked and savoured by all. Frequently this meal would be served in the front parlour, with father carving the joint, grace having been recited.

Since everyone dressed in their 'Sunday best' for the Sabbath, Monday was traditionally wash-day. Housewives would be out in force lighting fires under the brick and

Outhouses at Milton Bryan: a communal facility still in use.

lead-lined 'coppers' in the corner of the 'outhouse' which was more often than not a wood-constructed, pantiled building erected across the yard to the rear of cottages. This would house the copper and mangle, bungalow bath (a small aluminium bath with handles each end, which would be ceremoniously placed in front of the fire, partly filled by pans of hot water heated on the range, and used by everyone in succession, once a week). Gardening tools and equipment, father's bicycle, dried onions, large pots and pans would all adorn the outhouse.

Washing boiled in the copper and blue rinsed for added whiteness, would be hand-turned through the mangle and proudly pegged out on the line to dry – rows of billowing sheets, bolster and pillow cases, petticoats and other wearing apparel. Little wonder black was such a popular colour for ladies' garments of this era – it didn't show the dirt and required laundering less frequently than many of our modern-day clothes. Aprons and pinafores were worn by girls and women in the home, and at school, to protect and preserve garments.

If good weather prevailed, Tuesday would be ironing day. A heavy 'smoothing iron' would be heated on the range, and used to iron clothing which had been sprinkled with water and rolled to dampen prior to ironing. Often two irons would be used alternately, so no time was wasted waiting for the iron to reheat.

Making up beds using traditional bedding – feather pillows, sheets, blankets and bedspreads, shaking and beating rugs, sweeping floors, making fires, cleaning grates, repairing clothes, picking home-grown vegetables, cleaning, skinning and plucking poultry (rabbit, pigeon and chicken were the most commonly used meats), cooking, washing up enormous pots, pans and utensils, drawing water from the well, collecting and chopping wood! Little wonder the saying 'a woman's work is never done'! Babies to care for, children to supervise.

In poor households nothing was wasted. A nutritious meal could be made from entrails: pork brine, pork trotters, fried or stewed brains and giblets, boiled tongue, fried pigs chitterlings, (small intestines), black pudding made with blood, rice, etc., neck o'lamb stew and so on. Every meal contained meat, but the roast joint was the week's speciality, a luxury reserved for Sunday lunch. Left-overs would be utilised if possible, such as bread pudding made from stale bread, or otherwise fed to the poultry or pig, which most country families reared. Thrift ensured that a meagre income adequately sustained a large family.

Childbirth

In Victorian and Edwardian times families were large and there are several reasons which explain this. The absence of effective methods of birth control is the most obvious of these, but probably not the most important. There is no doubt that

Little mother! Circa 1900.
Photo: courtesy Frank Newstead

Victoria and Albert popularised child-rearing and family life, even as happened temporarily to a lesser extent in modern times with the marriage of Charles and Diana. Couples were proud of their families, and pride grew with family size. Women did not expect to work outside the home after marriage, and in fact there were many women who did not work prior to marriage, but remained at home with parents, helping the family, providing care and nursing where illness occurred, and helping run family businesses. Some young women were encouraged to work – to 'go into service' more often than not, – as parents found it difficult to accommodate them, but there was certainly an attitude that women should not have to labour – more prevalent possibly, among the middle classes. There were few openings for women in occupations other than the traditional ones such as teaching, domestic work, lace-making, millinery and in retailing (shop assistants). Industrial labour for women was not regarded with approval, and this situation did not change until the time of the Great War, when it became necessary for women to work in business and industry. However, even in the period between the wars, only five per cent of married women in this country worked outside the home. In certain professions there was a legal bar against the employment of married women, and other trades imposed restrictions. To the vast majority of husbands, the idea of working wives was totally unacceptable.

Possibly of greater importance still, was religious influence which was strong and widespread. Illegitimacy remained a disgrace, with moral standards reinforcing family ties and family life. Girls and boys had different roles to play in life, and girls were raised with the expectation that they would become wives and mothers. Even whilst the dual system of secondary education existed, girls at Secondary Modern schools would be taught Domestic Science which included cooking, laundering, housework and elements of mothercraft.

Marriage legitimised the sexual relationship, the couple created the family, children perpetuated the family name, and provided security for parents in old age.

'When my mother was a teenager she came to live in one of the workers' hutments which were built by the side of the newly-constructed railway line from London to Manchester and the north [near Milton Ernest]. This is when she met my

father and they married at the parish church of Neston in Cheshire (my mother and her parents having left Milton Ernest when the railway contract came to an end). My mother and father then returned to the village of Milton Ernest to make their home.

I was born on 28 January 1901 in a stone and thatched cottage in Milton Ernest. There were eleven children in the family, five boys and six girls. I was the fourth child. My father, Ernest, and my grandfather, George, were both born in Milton Ernest and both had been expert thatchers. My mother was the daughter of Eliza and William Swanborough. Her father, William, was a navvy ganger employed by a construction contractor.

It was customary in those days for the name of each child born to be entered into a family Bible. My sister still has our old family Bible and in it, in my mother's handwriting, are listed the names of all her children: Alfred, Eleanor, George William Swanborough, Walter Reginald, Eliza, Verdie Mary, Sylvia Alice, William Ernest, Irene Hope, Victor Ephraim, Dorothy Kathleen.

We were brought up in the Christian faith, prayers being recited at bedtime and before breakfast, regular attendance at church and Sunday School, and all the children christened and later confirmed.

In one corner of the inglenook in our cottage, the original bread oven had been removed and mother kept the baby's basket there, containing all the necessary bits and pieces [vest, nightgown, matineé coat, cap, socks, shawl, etc.]. The village vicar used to lend a "hamper" of baby clothes for newly-born babies, for a period of six weeks, and this hamper was fetched as soon as baby was born and returned in good condition at the allotted time.'

WALTER 'REG' PARROTT

Child-bearing was considered a natural event by all members of the family. An elderly friend once remarked to the author that he recalled getting up in the morning and being told by a brother that mother gave birth to another baby during the night. He wasn't even aware that she was pregnant!

Childbirth was a common-enough event, and women in each community assisted at births.

'Childbirth for me was like going to the toilet. One minute I'd be sitting on the chamberpot and the next minute there it was! My mother was often called out to help at births (and deaths). She wasn't trained, but she helped until the midwife came. People used to help one another. You'd save brown paper to put on the bed for the delivery. You couldn't risk making a mess of your white linen and making a lot of washing. There wasn't any plastic sheeting then, but brown paper was waterproof. They used to tie a piece of cloth or towels on the top end of the bed, to pull on when the contractions came.

I'd got a little money saved up when my time came and I could have gone into hospital. You had to be means-tested for that, so I would have had to pay. My mother thought it was a waste of money. "Save your money" she said "and have it at home". That's what I did.'

CONSTANCE INSKIP (neé Green)
Born 8 March 1901

Before the 1930s the majority of babies were born at home, as medical care was expensive; there would be a fee for the ambulance, and a fee for the hospital or doctor. Another factor was no doubt the security of home delivery, far more personal and intimate than hospitalisation. Chloroform was commonly used in hospital deliveries, which were then conducted with instruments. Traditions had their influence, and the vast majority of women would no doubt have preferred to give birth in the comfort of their own home. Throughout the first decades of this century, the situation did not change.

Who can imagine being in labour at night, with one's husband anxiously waiting downstairs (custom decreed that husbands be excluded from the proceedings), and one's children asleep in adjoining rooms! As pains intensified, biting onto a rolled cloth, whilst pulling on the cloths attached to the bed-head, were simple methods employed to deter or stifle screaming!

Illness

Victorian and Edwardian families were far more self-sufficient and less dependent on state provision than we in modern-day society, and during times of illness, many ordinary families had to resort to time-honoured remedies of their own concoction. Some of the traditional remedies for various ailments are as follows:

Leeching, to reduce swelling after injury.

Hot cokes dropped into water, called Cinder Water, as a cure for wind.

Goose-grease and brown paper applied to the chest for bronchitis and chest ailments.

Camphorated oil, olive oil and powdered mustard mixed and rubbed hot onto chest for bronchial ailments.

Kaoline Poultice applied to chest for coughs.

Bees-wax and liquid from stewed marshmallow leaves to make ointment for application to cuts and bruises, or Zam-Buk ointment, or rub in honey – a cure for all things.

Thermagine wool on chest for chesty coughs and respiratory disorders.

Close all windows and doors, put hot coals and gas-tar or sulphur onto the fire shovel to fumigate the cottage to prevent coughs and sneezes in the family.

Camphor hung in a linen bag around children's necks to ward off germs.

Toes soaked in urine, a cure for chilblains.

Roasted onion placed in a sock, applied to ears to ease aches.

Drink half a pint of rum, dress up well and go to bed to 'sweat it out', as a cure for 'flu.

Boil comfrey leaves and apply directly, to treat strains and sprains.

Put sultanas and sugar in a cloth and tie tightly, for teething babies to bite on.

Cook onions and make a white sauce. Eat whilst in bed, as

hot as possible, as a cure for a bad chest cold.

Rub chest and back with camphorated oil, for colds.

Inhale Wintergreen and boiling water, placing a towel over the head (or use Friars Balsam) for head colds.

Make a poultice by heating in a saucepan, yellow basilicon (an ointment made of wax, pitch and resin) and Epsom salts, wrap in a cloth and bind on, as hot as possible, with a bandage. For boils and carbuncles.

Heat linseed (obtainable from chemists) with water in a saucepan and put in a cloth. Place this poultice, as hot as possible, on the affected part. A cure for bad backs.

Nettles and dandelions were gathered from hedgerows. These were considered to be purifiers of the blood, and were boiled, sugar added, and then the mixture barrelled. After some time it would be bottled, and this made a delicious drink. It is known to have been used for the treatment of shingles.

Cough mixture could be made from onion, which would be sliced and placed in a large dish and raw sugar (Molasses) placed on top. This was then covered and left for a few hours. The syrup which was the onion juice and the sugar all mixed up, made a pleasant drink and an effective cough mixture.

Another remedy for ear ache would be to pop a potato into the 'range' and this would later be cut into half and one half placed in a woollen sock, knitted and kept for this purpose, and placed on the ear. The steam soon melted the wax and the ear could be washed out. This was less dangerous that syringing.

A treatment for 'tummy colds' was half a teaspoon of ginger added to a cup of hot water and one teaspoon of sulphur and of black treacle mixed in well. A teaspoon of this would be given at bed-time.

Well-known formulations could be purchased from the chemist, such as Melrose ointment for chilblains, or Scots Emulsion to keep colds at bay.

In the case of serious and contagious illnesses such as

Scarlet Fever or Diptheria, the patient was transferred to an isolation hospital, but Chicken Pox and Measles, common among children, meant that the patient would remain in bed.

Of course, in times gone by, no garden was complete without a Herb Garden and Comfrey, Marshmallow, Peppermint, Mint, Sage and Parsley were always to be found – among others – many of which are still used today for flavouring food. These herbs had other, medicinal, uses.

Comfrey was known as Knit-bone by the old time Romanies and was used for the treatment of bruises, sprains and fractures. The leaves were scalded and when cool enough for the patient to endure, the hot leaves were applied and bandaged with a soaked bandage. This was done at approximately two to three-hourly intervals during the day. The pain, swelling, and discolouration was considerably reduced.

Marshmallow leaves were gathered, boiled, strained and beeswax added. When cool the mixture would be packed into any of the smaller jars available. With this application, no bruise would ever become septic.

Peppermint was boiled and a particular quantity of sugar added to each pint of liquid. When cold this was bottled in empty wine bottles, corked and tied with string. During winter months this was a lovely remedy for a cold or for tummy upsets.

Sage was commonly used in the treatment of sore throats. The leaves were scalded and when cool enough, used as a gargle. This was safer than using a disinfectant, as if some were accidentally swallowed, it did no harm.

Mint and parsley were hung in bunches in windows, to deter flies. Parsley was considered 'good for the blood' and children were encouraged to wash and chew a sprig as often as they wished.

(COURTESY H S BROWN.)

Death and Bereavement

Births and deaths were, until well into the twentieth century, strictly family matters, largely dealt with within the privacy of the home. It was considered normal to die at home and those who died in hospital were usually brought home and laid in the living room in their coffin, which was placed on tressels often with carbolic soap placed beneath, to deter smells, and the coffin was left open. During three days or so prior to burial, family and friends would call to pay their respects, occasionally holding a 'wake' to comfort the near relatives of the deceased person. Curtains remained closed, with blinds pulled down. Relatives wore a black armband or a black diamond shape on their sleeve as a mark of mourning. Black clothing or subdued shades were worn as a mark of respect, and mourning jewellery, – frequently Jet – popularised by the Victorians, was still in use. A popular item of jewellery was the locket, into which would be placed a few strands of the deceased's hair. Cards and notepaper could be bought with black borders. In the hat trade, black dye was used on hats for funerals, particularly for royal funerals, when black would be required by a nation in mourning. Periods of mourning differed, but six weeks appears to have been the minimum period. This could be as long as one year, however. Infant mortality rates were still high, and among large families death in the family was sadly a not uncommon occurrence.

In many families, as an elderly person grew frail and death approached, garments to be worn in death would be selected and placed in a suitcase under the bed. Most ladies set aside a black hat, scarf and gloves to wear at funerals. The black veil was worn at the funeral by Victorian ladies, but eventually the hat succeeded the veil (though hats incorporating a partial veil were also popular at one time).

When death came, local ladies skilled in the task of laying out the dead would be called in. After placing the deceased person on the bed, the body would be washed completely, back and front, and a little packing material placed in the back-passage. A strip of cloth would be tied around the chin and head, to keep the mouth closed, and books or something similar, placed either side of the head to keep the face uppermost. If the eyelids would not remain closed, a cold penny (pennies of the day were large coins) would then be placed on the eyelid. The body would be dressed in the chosen clothing, or otherwise in white cotton (often a nightdress or a specially made gown with ruched neck). Arms were folded across the chest. Legs would be tied loosely with a bandage or strip of cloth at the knee and ankle. When the body had 'set', the hair would be combed neatly, and bandages removed. One expression in vogue in earlier times was that the deceased would 'go out clean', and this was a matter of great importance to all families.

It is estimated that after five hours the body would be rigid, and therefore preparations needed to be put in hand after death had been confirmed. The laying out task would take approximately an hour. The deceased would then be placed in the coffin or even left on the bed, for three days for viewing, prior to the funeral. The practice of placing something personal in the coffin appears to be a fairly recent one. Even children were not accompanied by personal possessions such as favourite toys. Rings and personal items of jewellery were sometime buried with the deceased. Alternatively they would be removed and placed in a box as a keep-sake.

Church bells were rung to mark a death in the community, and rung again when the funeral took place. The coffin was then placed on a hand-drawn cart or a bier, and the undertaker would walk in front with his bearers wheeling and pushing the cart behind him, and the mourners walking behind them.

'Wealthy people "went out" in a carriage pulled by black horses with plumes. I've heard of this, though I haven't seen

one. We had the most respectful funeral which anyone could afford. We sent them off in good style, and then the relatives and friends met afterwards and people took what they wanted from the house. Things were just shared out. Some people gave things away while they were alive. Well, there are things you don't want any more. There was a time when the Will was read after the funeral, during tea. Not everyone left a Will: some had nothing to give.'

CONSTANCE INSKIP (née Green)
Born 8.3.1901

Coffins had to be made up as quickly as possible so the deceased could be 'laid out', coffined and left at home. This was a task normally carried out by the local Wheelwright, Carpenter and Undertaker.

'There was one old woman in the village – always dressed in long black skirts – called Lizzy Darnell. She told me a secret just before she died. She said if ever I was laying anybody out and the features had gone, to get a drop of whisky in a saucer and dab it on the face to bring the features back. I said I'd rather drink it! There were two village ladies in Melchbourne who specialised in laying out the dead, Mrs Jackson and Mrs Reynolds.'

WINIFRED ALLAN

In warm weather laying out could be an unpleasant task because there were offensive smells. Once ready, however, the deceased was carefully placed in a specially made coffin, with white pillows and linings often made by the undertaker's wife.

'I started making coffins when I was eight or nine and at the age of nine or ten I was sent to South Wing [Bedford Hospital] to collect the body of a baby which had died. I went on foot, and carried the child's body all the way back to

Thurleigh. There were a lot of still-born and infant deaths in the early part of this century.

I often used to go at night, walking across the fields, to collect bodies. On one occasion when I'd been to Rutters Cottages by Twinwoods, my father-in-law to be said "Fred, you hadn't oughta ha' done that, you're creating a footpath by carrying a body over that field". It was generally thought, in the farming fraternity, that a by-law existed to this effect, enabling a right-of-way to be created if a body had been carried across land.'

FREDERICK WILDMAN

'When my father died in 1969, we wouldn't allow him to go to the Chapel of Rest. The coffin didn't come until the morning of the funeral and he laid on the bed until then.'

WINIFRED ALLAN

In the early years of this century, infant mortality rates were high, and the incidence of still-births, and it was not uncommon for several children in a family to be lost. Medical services had to be bought, and unless families contributed to medical schemes, self-treatment was the best alternative. Often the local chemist would be consulted for advice. Diptheria, Tuberculosis and Scarlet Fever were among the most fatal of illnesses.

In the early days, before the National Health Service came into being, most villages had a 'slate club' where each man paid in so much a month and if he were sick he had a doctor who issued a certificate so he could draw ten shillings a week from the Club. At the end of the year any money left in the Club was shared between members. Such Clubs were often run from Public Houses. There were the Friendly Societies such as the Hearts of Oak, which offered some cover too. A Luton resident recalls that when her mother was aged about thirty, around the turn of the century, many families had no money to bury the dead and Tommy Neville, the local undertaker, did the burial free of charge at the time, and allowed the family to pay a little each week thereafter, to cover the cost.

'The Friendly Society originated in 1820: the Stagsden Branch started in 1886. They were illegal in the first place, with secret meeting places and secret codes. This was similar in some ways to the Trade Union. It provided money for people when sick and death benefit when they died. It cost one shilling and ninepence per month in subscriptions. They drew ten shillings a week sick pay, reducing to five shillings after six months. The Provident Dispensary where medical relief was dispensed on payment of a small fee, occupied the impressive stone building erected in 1887 in St. Peter's Street, Bedford (now the Probation Office), then St. Peter's Green. Ten pounds was payable on death. There was an undertaker in Stagsden, who was also the wheelwright and carpenter, who arranged the funeral within three days of death. He charged ten pounds which was what people drew and all they could afford.'

HORACE WELCH

'When in 1948 the National Health Service came along we couldn't believe it. We were having lectures on it in the army but we still didn't believe it would ever happen. Free doctors, free dental treatment!' [From 1946, the Ministry of Health became responsible for providing free medical treatment for all: National Health Service Act 1946]

JOHN 'JACK' THORNE

'I was my parents' thirteenth child, but sadly only seven of their children survived childhood. One of my brothers had eating diabetes, one sister was burned to death whilst we were living in Dropshort. My mother had gone to fetch milk, and left the baby by the guarded fire, but a spark caught her gown and she had burned to death by the time mother returned. I think the others may have been stillborn.'

IVY FLUTE

'Our local wheelwrights, the Redmans, made farm carts and wheels, but they were also the undertakers. The dead were kept in the house then. Mr Redman had the bearers come with the bier and they put the coffin on it. Some had the service in the house and then went to the cemetery. They used to keep this bier in a corner of the churchyard and the undertaker fetched it and came to the deceased's home. It was usual to keep the dead for about three days before burial.'

STANLEY LOVELL

This generation of people never forgot their dead, and graves were tended with loving care, grass trimmed and fresh flowers arranged.

A funeral procession in Luton, circa 1908. Photo: Luton & Neighbourhood Illustrated, publisher T G Hobbs, circa 1910

31

'I cared for my husband for a long time before he died, which was a week before Christmas. He is always in my thoughts and when I get my ten pounds' Christmas bonus each year I buy five roses and five red carnations which I put in the church window by the Remembrance Book which bears his name.'

BEATRICE 'MAY' WEBB

Many children were victims of parental mortality. Mary Cooling (Jeffs) pictured above, aged approximately three years, (circa 1896) lost her mother in infancy and was raised by her paternal grandparents.

CHILDHOOD

CHILDHOOD

Introduction

At the turn of the century childhood was, in general, a stimulating experience of living in a large family unit with many brothers and sisters, and often with grandparents sharing the family home, or otherwise living nearby and having close contact. Maiden aunts often lived out their lives within the family, and since trades were continued in the time-honoured tradition, from father to son, it was common for several generations to occupy the same property. Rights over occupation of tied cottages were passed on from one generation to the next. Occupational and therefore geographical mobility are a more recent phenomenon, splitting families and leading to social isolation. Certainly in the period leading up to the first world war, children experienced greater psychological security, being surrounded by siblings and many relatives, and

Edrop Joseph Sharman, the Bolnhurst miller.
Photo: courtesy A Woodward.

mothers enjoyed greater support, being able to rely on parents, nearby relatives, and neighbours for help or advice in times of need. A typical country family are depicted in the following photographs – the Sharmans of north Bedfordshire.

Maurice Sharman, born in 1913, and his cousin Gwenneth Sharman. Maurice followed his father, Edrop, into milling. Photo: courtesy A Woodward

Each member of the family made his or her contribution towards the maintenance of the unit. Young children might be expected to feed the animals (hens, pigs and the like), collect eggs, fetch water from the well or shared outside tap, carry washing water upstairs for parents, polish shoes, collect firewood, and for older children, care for younger brothers and sisters, the girls often repairing clothing or making clothes for the children. Work was an accepted element in the order of things. Boys would often commence

Mrs Elizabeth
Sharman, mother
to Ernest, Charlie
(emigrated to
Canada), Aunt Liz
(a Nurse), Kate and
Edrop (Maurice's
father).
Photo: courtesy
A Woodward

work at the age of nine, when they were considered old enough to assist their father on the farm and in the family business, and to help with the harvesting. The transition from school to work at the age of twelve or thirteen was a natural progression, and did not present problems for youngsters who were already initiated and experienced in the traditional occupations.

A substantial proportion of any young person's income would be assimilated into the family's budget, to ease the

The Sharman family and friends pose for a photograph, taken by Mr Rastrick, in the field behind Oxford Farm, Keysoe Row East. Circa 1915.
Left to right: Mrs Losemore (Aunt Liz), Maurice Sharman (baby) on 'Kit', Mrs E J Sharman (Aunt Polly), Elijah Brown (lived in what is now Toby Cottage), Mr E Sharman, Gwen Sharman (baby) on 'Prince', Mrs M Sharman, Mrs Elizabeth Sharman (Granny), Norman Rolls on 'Blossom', Miss Chidell, Alice Wilson (later Mrs Clark). Photo: courtesy A Woodward

Maurice Sharman pictured in retirement. He died in 1987. Photo: courtesy A Woodward

burden of providing for so many. Children could make 'pocket' money whilst at school by collecting and selling such things as firewood, wild flowers, acorns (used for pig food), nuts and wild berries, gleans for feeding to the hens, sparrow catching, lace-making and straw plaiting.

A child was regarded as an adult in the making and less as an individual in a unique stage of development, with distinct needs and rights. The adult provided the role model, and the child aspired to the behavioural patterns and life-style of his/her parents and elders.

The Victorian lifestyle was still emulated by more affluent families whose children were entrusted to the care of resident staff – the nanny and governess with whom they frequently formed a close rapport, developing affectionate and enduring relationships.

For some children, however, the loss of parents through illness or accident led to an upbringing with grandparents or other relatives or alternatively, in an orphanage. One such establishment existed in Beech Hill, Luton, in the early years of this century. Children from the orphanage were dressed in uniform clothing and as a result, were easily recognisable as orphans – a predicament which some believe led to discrimination.

It has been suggested that such youngsters were dealt with more harshly at school than were others whose parents were more ready to spring to their defence.

A number of migrants were sent overseas to Commonwealth countries from the Beech Hill and other institutions, in particular to Canada, South Africa and Australia, for reasons which are not entirely clear. The policy of resettlement has been criticised in recent times, since the resultant social problems have been given publicity. Forced resettlement may well have been less for altruistic reasons than for the purposes of providing a cheap source of labour and easing the burden on the State of providing for the distressed youngsters. A movement now exists in this country, for the purpose of reuniting many of these individuals – now elderly people – with their 'roots' and facilitating contacts with lost relatives. Child migrants were required in some instances, to change their names, and brothers and sisters were frequently dispatched to different locations.

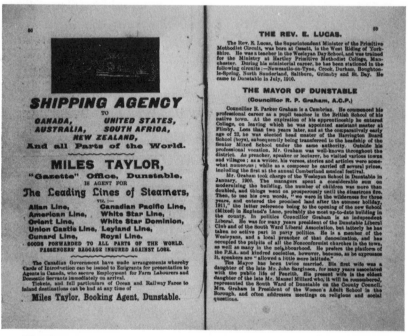

The Commonwealth: encouraging emigration and population growth in 1913.
From Year Book & Directory, 1913. Courtesy: Dunstable Gazette and Mr E Baldock.

Growing Up in Dunstable

'I was born on 1 July 1905 and was the youngest of eight children. My father owned a bakery in Dunstable and this was where I was born and brought up, at 44 High Street South.

Elsie England in the arms of her father, photographed in 1905 with her mother, brothers and sisters in front of their family home and bakery at 44 High Street South, Dunstable.

My father employed someone to help at the bakery – Albert Howe – but my eldest brother did most of the deliveries, by horse and cart. I had a bread round of my own at one time, delivering from a basket. This was just to help out: I didn't want to work in the bakery.

My childhood was a very happy one. My mother and father worked as one, helping each other. They really worked well together. My first school was Burr Street [now called Icknield], and I transferred to Britain Street School which is now called Priory School, when I was eleven. I really can't remember unhappy times. Most of all I liked roller skating.

Children at Britain Street School (now known as Priory School). Elsie England appears in the second row back, and fourth from left.

I learned to skate on the A5! We used to skate down Half Moon Hill – providing there was nothing coming. There used to be a pub at the bottom called the Half Moon. It is still there but no longer a public house. We often used to play with hoops and tops: you could whisk them along with a piece of string, and keep them going for ages. They needed new pegs every once in a while and we used to go to "Old Joe" who was the shoe repairer. He did a lot of things for children, mending toys and so on.

Dad used to take us out occasionally, usually on Thursday afternoons which was early closing. We'd go to Batford [near Harpenden] to visit mother's relatives, by horse and waggon. My grandmother lived in a nearby hamlet called Coldharbour: she did hats at home. People of our station didn't used to go away for holidays in those days. I didn't see the sea until I was fourteen!'

ELSIE ENGLAND

A Village Smallholder's Daughter

'I was one of eight children, and my parents had moved to Wootton from their family home in Marston Moretaine. During my childhood my father was a smallholder, who earned his living selling eggs, chickens, ducks and so on, from a pony and trap, on village rounds. I occasionally went with him. He also supplied hotels in Bedford, which was a paricularly good outlet for the fresh butter which his mother made, on her farm at Marston. In my younger days Wootton was a self-supporting community, with all necessities being locally-produced. Rabbits were shot locally and sold for about sixpence, and there was always a plentiful supply. My father also kept pigs at his smallholding in Bedford Road and so dealt in bacon, home-made sausages and black pudding, which my mother made.'

CONSTANCE ROBINSON

A Childhood Spent in Milton Ernest

'At our family home all water had to be either collected in a wooden barrel, a water butt, or drawn from the local well on a windlass and chain or rope. Outside the front door of the cottage stood a crude bench; this is where my brothers and I had our daily wash, summer and winter alike, come hail, rain or shine. Our toilet was equally crude, being a hole in the ground with a seat over the top, emptied annually until 1913, when a new law took effect, requiring the use of the bucket system.

Father kept several pigs and cultivated two roods of allotments where he grew vegetables and cereals. At harvest time the wheat he grew was mown with a scythe, stooked, threshed and the grain taken to the mill to be ground into flour.

At the age of ten I developed scarlet fever, a common complaint amongst children at that time, and I was sent to Clapham isolation hospital, which was about three miles from our home. I was taken by the fever van, which was a horse-drawn vehicle with two small windows in the rear. I remained in hospital for six weeks. No visitors were allowed during this time and anyone who called had to stand on a wooden plank fixed to the outside wall, and peer through the windows to see the patient. It is said that the plank remains there to this day.

Pocket money had to be earned in my childhood days, by collecting acorns and selling them (for one shilling a bushel), picking primroses and violets for decorations, picking mushrooms, searching for discarded horseshoes and ploughshares, cow-keeping by the roadside, bird scaring and sparrow catching.

A favourite winter evening occupation during my young days was the cutting up of old and left-off clothing, often from jumble sales, with which we made rag rugs. Most sought after were red hunting jackets, the material from which could be used for patterning, to enliven the rug. There was no TV or radio then, just the steady ticking of the grandfather clock. From August onwards, straw or corn dollies were made and various ornaments to decorate the corn stacks. Some farmers took great pride in their rickyards.'

WALTER 'REG' PARROTT

An MP's Family

'My grandfather on the Wells side of the family died before I was born, in 1913 to be precise, and my grandmother lived at Castle Close [Bedford], which is now the Cecil Higgins Museum. The rooms are now restored and look much as they did when she lived there.

My maternal grandparents lived in India, where grandfather was a judge, and they retired to Bedford when grandfather was only about forty-seven. Many people did likewise, returning from the colonies to settle either in Bedford or Cheltenham, in order to educate their children.

*Victorian drawing room in the Cecil Higgins Art Gallery and
Museum, Bedford. Photo: courtesy The Trustees, The Cecil
Higgins Art Gallery, Bedford, England.*

Grandfather having lost most of his money on poor investments, the couple came to live in a small house in Felmersham in their latter days and mother kept an eye on them. They did not influence my upbringing to any great extent.

Children of Sir Richard and Lady Wells.
Left to right: Top: Thomas, George, James, David.
Front: Charles, Sarah, Mary, Oliver, Christopher

'I was a twin, and the youngest of nine children. My early years at Felmersham Grange, where I was born, were extremely happy and memorable, living with such a large family amid the constant activity and excitement generated by older brothers and their friends.

'Our time spent at Felmersham Grange was one of security, contentment and happiness. My mother had been an accomplished artist in her younger days, having studied at the Slade School of Art under Bryan Shaw. Father, Sir

Richard Wells, went into parliament the year I was born and was an energetic and busy man but one who enjoyed family life and liked being at home. He never spent more time living in London than was absolutely necessary, and always looked forward to returning home.

Felmersham Grange, birthplace of Oliver Wells.

There was something special about Felmersham. It was a very happy home with youthful days spent playing and swimming in the river which skirted the grounds. We used to have relays and what we called the 'Felmersham Test' which involved swimming a certain distance and which, once accomplished, meant that one could go out in the boat. Father built a squash court and tennis court so we could enjoy games.

'My twin sister and I shared a governess until I went to Preparatory School at Little Appley on the Isle of Wight at the age of eight.

'My governess was a tiresome old woman, but Miss

Rear view of Felmersham Grange, looking across the river.

Chapman, our Nurse and Housekeeper, was very dear to us
and was regarded by us all as belonging to the family. She
died during the war and I was sorry not to be able to see her
prior to her death.'

OLIVER WELLS

A Country Girl

'I was born at Knotting Green. My father and his father, were
also born there, near the church in Knotting. Father spent all
his working life on Green Farm, owned by Mr Pike. We lived
in a tied cottage: there weren't any private properties at that
time. Of the six children in our family, one died at the age of
twelve with appendicitis.

There were some weird remedies around in those times.
When we were children and had chilblains they would say
"dip your toes in the pot" and you know, it did the trick! Joe
Berry, who lived in the cottages, – the chimney sweep, – his
boy had whooping cough and they gave him fried mice.

Knotting Green, 1956

Winifred Allan (centre) and sisters. Elsie (right), died in 1925

We used to go sparrow catching as children, and made sparrow pie. There was a sparrow club at one time and I have been round the church with a net and bamboo canes, catching them along the ivy. They had to be plucked, but were quite a delicacy. Lambs tails were another tasty dish. They could be fried or put in a pie. The shepherd took them to the Swan at Sharnbrook and they had lambtail supper. We never had a pub in Knotting.

I had an exceedingly happy childhood. Schooldays were happy, and there was a season for everything. We would be out collecting cowslips and dandelions for wine, blackberrying and mushrooming and acorning for pig food. We used to visit Mrs Smith's sweet shop, where we could get linseed and cholordine. By and large we had a very carefree childhood. We could wander miles over fields and no-one interfered with us. We were not scared of anything and we'd go out early morning and only come home at lunchtime to eat. No-one had a holiday as such, not to go away.'

WINIFRED ALLAN

Knotting Green Postman, circa 1920.

A Family of Fourteen

'I was born in Clapham on 16 June 1908 and we lived at The Warren. My father was a gardener and grave-digger. For ten years of his life he worked solely as a grave-digger at Bedford Cemetery, but later worked in the Clapham churchyard, where Mr Tinsley was the undertaker at the time. He was paid ten shillings for digging a grave. I was actually born in a terrace of four houses called Tavistock Cottages. These cottages had three bedrooms, which was just as well as there were twelve children in the family. My mother was a very small person, who suffered with bronchial asthma.

We children slept head to foot, several in one bed. There were four girls, one of whom died. The six boys occupied a second bedroom. There had been twin boys but they died as babies, or possibly at birth – I'm not sure, – as this was before I was born. The boys frequently squabbled and battled for space, but mother would go up and sort them out. She knew how to put a stop to it! My sister was thirteen years older than me and we shared a room together.

My parents were very poor and dad was glad to get a job grave digging now and again because his wage as a gardener was only ten shillings a week. Mother often bought secondhand clothes from a trader who called round on a Saturday night. Most things were brought to the door then. The fish merchant came twice a week with fresh fish.

We children sometimes shopped for mother before going to school, as the shops opened at 7 am. On the odd occasions when mother had to shop in Bedford she was sometimes fortunate to be offered a lift by Lady Ampthill who lived at Oakley House. He was one of the elite but she was a lovely lady. (He was a nephew of the Duke of Bedford, at that time.) We children thought ourselves lucky if we were given a lift home on the milk float!'

GWENDOLINE BROWN

A Childhood Spent in Goldington

'I was born in a thatched cottage in Cricket Lane, Bedford, in 1909. My parents moved to School Yard when I was about three, which is at the back of Barkers Lane and near to Goldington School. There were three of us children. Father was a sheet metal worker at Allens, as was his father.

Winifred Burton pictured in 1910 with her mother and Uncle Joe, mother's brother, at their thatched cottage in Cricket Lane, Goldington.

As children we found plenty of things to do to amuse ourselves. We used to go round the fields, go to chapel, and play on the green. My father used to play cricket on the green many years ago and there used to be stalls there then, while the cricket was being played. We were often given a glass of lemon with ice cream in it, which was a real treat. The village feast, which was held on the green of course, was a great occasion for us children. There were three caravans and the steam engine, the traction engine to provide the power. It

*Winifred Burton
photographed at
fifteen months,
whilst living at
8 St. Lawrence
Street, Bedford.*

*stank to high heaven. There was spit rock and roast potatoes
and we could go for a penny ride on the fairground. There
were penny rolls and coconut shies, and dolls and things as
prizes. We thought it was marvellous. They were the
highlights of the village year; we didn't have much else. Our
play things were balls, marbles, hoops, skipping ropes and so
on. We used to play hide and seek in the fields and there were
events organised by the chapel, such as races and a search
activity where sweets were scattered in the long grass for the
children to find. Playing in the fields was very enjoyable.*

*I had to go and fetch fresh milk every morning from
Ballinghalls. There was a brook through the green which was
filled in, but they used to grow watercress there. The vicarage
was nearby. There was a little bridge to be crossed to get to
chapel and another to get to Ballinghalls Farm. The
blacksmith used to be at the bottom of Cricket Lane and we
children used to love watching them shoe the horses. Of
course, much of this has changed now. The village green isn't
at all as it used to be.*

*My mother suffered a stroke when I was seven and her
youngest child was only a year old. She was paralysed on one*

*Winifred
Burton aged
three years.*

side. I had to struggle to get her on the bed and run next door
for grandmother. From that time onwards I had to nurse and
help her. She was a Christian woman, a beautiful woman, my
mother. She had been in service before she married my father.
In spite of her stroke, she lived to be sixty-seven, and died in
1957.'

WINIFRED BURTON

A Farmer's Son

'I was born at Manor Farm, Knotting, in 1907. My father was
a local man and a farmer. My mother lived in Peterborough
before her marriage, but had relatives in Sharnbrook and so
was no stranger to this area. They had six children, two boys
and four girls.

  I cannot remember a time when I was not made to work on
my father's farm. From the age of seven I had always helped

John Campion's grandfather, Henry, pictured in Tavistock Street, Bedford, circa 1915. He farmed at Bletsoe, Castle Farm, and died in his mid eighties.

at harvest time, carting corn and leading the horses. It was a mixed farm, and I looked after the animals and did almost everything that father did. It was always my ambition and intention to return to the farm after leaving school, and this is what I did, at the age of sixteen.

JOHN CAMPION

A Boyhood Spent in Luton

'I was born in 1900 at 31 Ashton Street, Luton, which was later called Gillam [Street] because of confusion with Ashton Road [named after James Gillam who founded the Mission in Ashton Street in 1885]. My father was a bonnet maker (according to his marriage certificate) and worked for Robinson & Butt, 38/40 Bute Street. My mother had worked for Rudd's the well-known confectioners, pastry cooks and bakers. They had shops in Chapel Street, Church Street and Park Street. The shop in Park Street was originally a pub called 'Ye Olde Wheel Plough' and the pub sign was used as a

motif on the cake boxes and bags. They were the premier confectioners, and she worked there from a child until quite late in life. She served in the shop and also used to prepare the hams, removing the skins and so on. It was a regular thing in Luton for women to work after marriage. She had six children (seven actually, but one died at birth), two of these were girls and both are still alive and older than me – one was ninety-four in May 1989 and the younger one ninety-one in August 1989.

Frank Chapman in his mother's arms, with brothers and sisters. Circa 1901.

Mother was very jocular, and father was so serious you know. He wouldn't come on holiday, but would give us all we wanted and more besides. If mother wanted a fur coat he would spend a hundred pounds or so without blinking an eye. He would rig her out with muffs with fur tails, fur coat, fur hat. He would spend his money, but not on himself. He was a very studious man, who had been to St. Matthews Elementary School but was really self-educated. He could read Egyptian hieroglyphics, was a musician, and organist. He was always studying, reincarnation and all sorts of things he was interested in. He wanted me to go to university but I am afraid I let him down.

My grandfather was an umbrella maker with a business in John Street. He was very well-known locally being tall and

Waller Street Boys School, Luton.
The following caption accompanying the photograph, appeared in the Luton & Neighbourhood Illustrated, publisher T G Hobbs circa 1910:
'The attitude of the public towards education has changed considerably since the establishment of a general compulsory system in 1870 . . . Over 3,000 boys have passed through the school and many are now occupying important positions in the town and in other localities. The school has done excellent work and has gained a wide-spread reputation'.

The Grand Theatre in Waller Street, Luton, opened by Mrs Langtry in 1898. It could accommodate 1,000 people and was fitted with a 'modern ventilating system'.
Photo: Luton & Neighbourhood Illustrated, publisher T G Hobbs, circa 1910.

upright with snow white hair and beard, who always wore a top hat and tail coat. Well-off people had their favourite umbrellas re-covered rather than buying new ones, as the "sticks" were all individually designed. Lady Ludlow from Luton Hoo always had her umbrella covered in denim. He called them the "Gentry". Many people chose gingham for their umbrellas, and my father would always say "where's my gingham" when referring to his umbrella.

My second school was Waller Street School (page 57). Waller Street was an amusing, interesting street. There was a school, a medical institute, swimming baths, assembly hall, two public houses, a chapel, shops, a saddler's and a smithy. It ran parallel with the main street, close to the railway station.

I worked at the Grand Theatre in Waller Street as a programme and chocolate boy whilst at school, to dodge music lessons – you know what boys are. This was the only theatre in Luton then, although there were several picture houses. I was taught all the songs of the day from the London shows, the Music Halls. Oddie was my music teacher's name, and he was the headmaster's son. He was a lovely speaker but not a teacher with whom I found favour. I saw him after his retirement but you know I couldn't bring myself to tell him what I thought of him. He was such a sorry sight that I felt more like crying for him.

When I was about seven my mother took me to see Buffalo Bill. He came over to perform for the king, and afterwards the circus came to Luton with a menagerie. It was a fine sight to see the Red Indians. It was held opposite Wardown Park.'
[Buffalo Bill (William F Cody) brought his Wild West Show on tour to many European cities from 1897, thrilling audiences with his romanticised portrayal of life in America's Wild West. Obviously an unforgettable spectacle.]

FRANK CHAPMAN

A Country Boy

'I was born at Hessett near Bury St. Edmunds, Suffolk, my mother being a Suffolk woman, but my father was born in Bedfordshire. They had three children, two boys and a girl. My brother, the last-born, died of meningitis when he was four or five.

I was born in 1916 and my father was a soldier in the Royal Fuseliers during the First World War. After demobilisation he went back to general farm work. My mother was a cook. She worked for Franklins the coal merchants at one time and was also with Lady Penn in Bedford in the Clapham area, I believe.

I lived with my maternal grandmother in Suffolk until I was nearly five. This was when father came out of the Forces and wanted to return to live in Bedfordshire. I got a lot of favours from my grandmother and she treated me very well, but the time came when father had got a job and settled down and felt that I needed discipline. It hadn't been easy for father to find work, being an invalid, but he eventually found a job at Mr Daniel's farm, Brewers Hall, Great Barford. This was just off the St. Neots' Road.

I can remember visiting my grandmother, Elizabeth Constant, at one time as a boy, with torn trousers. She said "I'm your grandmother, now get them off", so I handed them over for repair. She used them as a pattern and before I left she had machined me another pair! Having raised ten children and having lost her husband prematurely, she was a busy woman. She was the local lace-making representative. She produced designs which were circulated to out-workers – pillow lace-makers – and collected in their finished work from the villages to sell to Braggins. I still have some of the lace which she herself made.

My favourite occupation as a boy was stealing moorhen's eggs. These are beautiful and so are plovers' eggs. The first plovers eggs of the season go to royality. They always lay four on the ground and they are well camouflaged. The eggs are

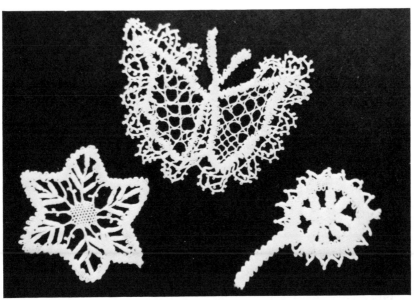

Lace motifs made by Bill Constant's grandmother, Elizabeth Constant.

An example of crochet lace, made by Elizabeth Constant.

pointed and when they are rotated by the hen, to point towards the middle, they are then addled, the hen has started to sit on them and they are no longer good for eating.

I enjoyed country life. It was a great thing to go and search out the various types of butterflies and moths. We are losing a lot on that score, it is becoming a very selfish society. More value is put on paper money and materialism, but there is so much more in life, that is how I look at it.

My parents kept poultry and goats. Father believed goats' milk was superior to cows' milk. There was no salmonella then. We milked these goats and mother made goats' butter and cheese. The French do a lot of it. We had a few pigs. There was life there all the time in that place. Father took all the rough when he came home from work, but mother saw to this while father worked. I took over when father got bad and couldn't do it.

My dad helped me to become interested in nature, and I would call myself a conservationist. Mother was very interested in horses and I used to ride as a boy. An aunt

Bill Constant's only sister, Phyllis, who died of consumption.

taught me to ride. You wouldn't be allowed a catapult by my father, to shoot a bird. His point of view was if a bird attacked a fruit then the fruit is no use to you because it is the maggot in it which the bird wants and not the fruit itself. He would demonstrate this by taking an apple off the tree, cutting it open and saying "there is the answer". I think it is a pity that more people do not have such a love of nature.

My sister, Phyllis was a nurse: she never married. We shared out parents' home [in Renhold] after their death. I promised her this, I said if I marry you will still have a home, which she would, and I said I shall not be any influence either way, which I would not. I thought too much of her. Really speaking, we were a very close knit family, something my mother always wanted. Mother and father were great parents and when you have got this in the family you cannot go far wrong.'

WILLIAM CONSTANT

Growing up in Bedford

Irene Cornwell's great grandparents, Mr & Mrs Litchfield (mother's grandparents). Note the headwear, typical indoor wear in draughty houses in early Victorian times.

'I was actually born in Dudley Street, Bedford, in 1910 but my parents later moved to Bower Street, near the embankment. Mother was a Bedfordian and her family were business people who lived in Chandos Street before she married. Her maiden name was Thompson and her married name Crowsley. My great grandparents were called Litchfield, and great grandfather was blind. My maternal grandfather, Mr Thompson, had a coal truck on Bedford

Granny and Grandpa Thompson, with Irene's mother and her two brothers, Arthur and Charles.

railway and did a coal round with a horse and cart. They also sold coal in the railway yard. It was usual for people to come in for a bucket of slack coal for threepence. On St. Thomas's Day the elderly people living at the Bedford Almshouses were given a St. Thomas's loaf of bread. Grandfather scrubbed one of his coal carts which had a false, clean, bottom put in it, and he delivered these loaves around. My mother lived to be one hundred.

My father was an engineer in the army. He was due to be posted to France and was working at the time on [building] a hospital in Sandwich, Kent. There was an epidemic of

Irene Cornwell's mother, who lived to be one hundred.

influenza and he died from this. The last time I saw him was when he was on leave and came home for two or three days, before going to France. He brought me a magnificent China doll.

In my younger days the regatta was a really special occasion, a regular day out. I would go across Russell Park to the embankment to make sure of a seat, and mother came later with her parasol to sit and watch the world go by. After that there was an ox roast on the river. There were boats for hire from Cheethams, who had two big houses by the river. The river was always a big attraction. My mother said it was frozen over for weeks at one time and the chestnut vendors were trading from their trolleys, there were fruit stalls, and people were actually ice skating. A real picture postcard scene. My mother had vivid memories of old Bedford. Not so many years ago Bedford Hospital North Wing was a workhouse for people on Parish Relief, which was only five shillings a week. The workhouse offered nightly lodgings for vagrants and other unfortunates, and also took in orphaned children. Mother used to talk of the cattle market which was held on the site of the Palace in the High Street, where people came bringing their animals in droves from the villages. The High Street was no more than a cart track then'

EDITH 'IRENE' CORNWELL

A Forester's Son

'I was born in a charity cottage – Milton Bryan Charity that is – and my parents later moved to an estate cottage. This was one built with no front door, as they say the Duke of Bedford at the time didn't like looking at women talking at their front doors!* The house had the Duke of Bedford's crest on it and the date it was built – I think it was around 1905. My father was a woodman, a forester on the Woburn estate. He used to

[* but more likely cleverly designed to avoid draughts]

*Thatched and weather-boarded cottage, birthplace of Chris Creamer.
The original boarding was carried out during his childhood, to stop
damp penetration.*

*fell trees for timber, keep the woods tidy, mow the rides –
that's clearing pathways through the woods for riders – clean
ditches out. About sixty worked in the Woods Department –
the Forestry Department. Now there are about six. The woods
were extensive and still are.*

*You had to work on the estate or on one of the farms on the
estate to get an estate cottage. On Tuesdays local people were
allowed to go into the park and pick up wood for their own
personal use, but hadn't to break any off the trees.*

*My mother played the organ at the local church from the
age of nine, the Milton Bryan Methodist Church that is.
Mother had six children.*

*My grandfather, Levi Creamer, my father's father, worked
on Manor Farm, which went with the Battlesden estate.
Battlesden House was built in 1864 on the outskirts of*

Levi Creamer working at Manor Farm, which belonged to the Battlesden Estate. Circa 1916.

Battlesden village near Woburn. It was built for Sir Edward Page-Turner and was a beautiful Elizabethan house. In 1885 it was bought by the Duke of Bedford – Duke Herbrand – and razed to the ground. Only the stable block and gatehouse remain [and the village is now classified as deserted].

My grandmother, Mrs Clark – mother's mother – always lived in Milton Bryan. She was born on St. Valentine's Day. She was taught needlework at a young age by Lady Inglis and the Misses Inglis in the little school at Milton Bryan which the Inglis family endowed. She made herself a new dress, by hand, for her ninetieth birthday, and lived to be ninety-seven.

While I was at school my nights and Saturdays were spent on the farm – sixpence a week. When I was about ten or eleven I started working on the farm. I didn't enjoy school. The bloke

I used to sit next to at the school got [to be] a big noise in ICI Chemicals you know. He was coached at the rectory by the parson.'

CHRISTOPHER CREAMER

Mrs Clark, Chris Creamer's maternal grandmother, who lived to be ninety-seven.

The Rag and Bone Merchant's Child

'I was born at Radwell, a hamlet near Felmersham, in February 1916. My father was a rag and bone man. I was his thirteenth child. My eldest brother was born out of marriage, and he took my mother's maiden name of Cook. I had four other brothers and one sister. The others died. My mother suffered much ill-health.

'Raggy' Lawson, Ivy Flute's father, a Marine Dealer.

Mother says I had a lot of nursemaids when I was young as, being wartime, we had soldiers billetted with us. They nursed me and played with me and dressed me up in their helmets – according to mother. When I was three my parents moved to Stevington and took on a smallholding called Ashtons, which was two miles out of the village. This was the distance I walked to and from Stevington School each day. Whilst we were there I had scarlet fever. My parents returned to Radwell when I was nine, and father bought a cottage next to the ones he already owned, and which he had bought from his mother. His first cottage was condemed but he fitted a galvanised roof over the thatch, to render it habitable.

Father was a rag and bone man and [later a] scrap metal merchant and everyone locally knew him as "Raggy Lawson". On my marriage certificate he is described as a "Marine Dealer". When he was sixteen he was involved in an accident at the shoe factory in Rushden where he worked, and as a result of this accident he lost an arm. In spite of this, he was very energetic and enterprising. He depended upon us children for help with his work though, and as the boys grew up and left home, I had to shoulder the responsiblity.

During my childhood I had to help my parents in many ways. Father used to do house rounds, buying rags, bones, rabbit skins, iron and scrap metal – anything which was saleable. He disposed of his scrap merchandise through John Fame & Sons in Beckett Street, Bedford, the bones being sold to glue manufacturers and so on. He used horses and carts and so I was brought up with horses and frequently went with him on his rounds. In later years he sold direct to Larkins and Sons who collected from the yard at our home.

I kept the horses on the side of the road in the summer and grazed them in the field. I cut chaff, pulped mangel wurzels by hand (these are like swedes but larger and more watery). These had to be mixed with the chaff (the corn straw) and corn, to make horse feed. I took the horses to Mr Roughhead's the blacksmith in Milton Ernest, to be re-shod. This was opposite the Queens Head public house. I had to take a day off school for

Ivy and her brothers tending the horses.

this, and another day off each Friday to do the housework. I was allowed time off school because of mother's illness.

When I was eleven I had to help father in the rag house when I came home from school, sorting whites, coloureds, and woollens, bagging them up separately and rolling the bales up onto the trolley to be taken to Bedford. When I was twelve I drove a horse and four-wheeled trolley into Bedford, and delivered to John Fames. Some Saturday mornings I had to go to Riseley to dismantle machinery which Father had bought – ploughing gear, engines and so on – and load them onto the trolley. Father, with his disability, needed all the help I could give. Another of my tasks was to collect rents from father's three rented cottages in Radwell. This totalled twelve shillings. When electricity became available father offered to have it connected for another sixpence a week, but the tenants couldn't afford it. Everyone used paraffin lamps then and candles to take to bed. It was common for families to go to bed at 6pm because they couldn't afford the lighting and heating.

Mother used to skin and gut rabbits, as rabbit was the main meat in those days. Father sometimes bought a sheep's head and this was stewed with vegetables to make "shackles". This was considered to be quite a delicacy, together with the lights (brains) and tongue. Occasionally we had stuffed and baked bullock's heart. All the cooking was done on the cooking range, of course – no gas or electric ovens then.

Our home was much like that of Steptoe & Son, but perhaps not quite so bad on the inside.

I had to work hard for my father but with his disability he needed all the help he could get. I had a good relationship with dad and he sometimes took me to rugby matches and whist drives, and he used to stay on with me for the dance afterwards. After I married he used to come out with us on Saturday nights. All we needed was a "latch-lifter" – six pence for our first round of drinks – and the rest of the evening cost us nothing as long as we won game upon game of cribbage, which we frequently did.'

IVY FLUTE

Life in Newnham Street, Bedford

'I was born on Boxing Day 1894 in St. Cuthbert's Parish, Bedford and I was the last of eleven children. My father had his own decorating business and I think our family were comfortably-off. I grew up in a large house in Newnham Street, which had four bedrooms, two reception rooms downstairs and a lobby. Mother's pantry was as big as a large room, and there was always something good in it, something home-cooked. Father had a double barrelled shotgun and a "shoot", and frequently brought home ducks, pheasants and pigeons. Many people shot for food then, and hare and partridge pie were very popular. Father cleaned, skinned and prepared his catch. He also fished occasionally. Mother had a big, round stew jar which was always stocked and on the go. She cooked on the kitchen range then, as there was no gas stove, just a black iron, nickel-plated shining monster of a range which mother spent hours cleaning. It was God help us if we spilled anything on it. There were two tables to be set at mealtimes, to seat all the family. Father officiated and in fact whatever father said was law, and mother would always say in reply to a request "You'll have to ask your father". If we children giggled at the table, which occasionally happened, then father would send us out the back door until we had composed ourselves and could return to the table.

Always after tea, we had to change our shoes for cleaning and putting under the cupboard ready for the next day. Slippers were worn inside the house. One of my brothers did the shoes and one the knives. We girls did forks, spoons and cruets. The chores were shared among us.

On Saturdays we had a ha'penny each to spend. If it was a wet day the older ones went out to spend it and took an order for the rest. The confectionary shop was opposite our house. We often had Spanish cakes on Saturday and Sunday, and delicious Hot Cross Buns were brought around by bike on Good Fridays. I think I was spoilt by my older brothers and sisters: some of them were already at work as I grew up. On Sundays mother took the girls and father the boys, for a walk and we met up at the Fox and Hounds in Goldington. There we children sat outside in the garden where we shared a glass of ginger beer and ate tea biscuits, half of one each.

Mother always made her own Christmas puddings, six or seven of them, and they were kept on top of the dresser, in the copper, until Christmas. We used to hang up our stockings before going to bed on Christmas Eve and the next morning they would be filled with sweets, nuts, oranges, apples and occasionally bananas, and holly.

On high days and holidays we had a fire in the front room, but we lived for most of the time in the kitchen, where mother and father sat nearest the fire and the rest of us sat around the three tables in the room. We weren't barred from using the "front room" but it wasn't heated.

Life was quite uneventful in Newnham Street, but on one occasion a neighbour opposite hung herself in a workshop. We were all there in our nightdresses peering excitedly from the bedroom windows, trying to see what was going on!

One of my sisters – Dolly – suffered long-term illness, and frequently had fits. We were all brought up to be caring towards her, and would watch over her during her fits, and take her inside the house to recover if she were taken ill whilst playing. There were homes for the sick and for the poor, but mother and father wouldn't allow her to go, and came in for much criticism by the church-goers who felt they were doing the wrong thing. We children grew up to be thoughtful and caring though, and Dolly lived until the age of forty-seven.'

HILDA HAYDEN

A Lace-Maker's Daughter

'My mother lived in one of the four Yeoman's Cottages at Chennell's Farm, [Wootton], then owned by Mr Frossell, and after her marriage, moved to Cause End Road in Wootton, where I was born in 1900, next door to the Star Public House and the shop. This property no longer exists. When I was a year old my parents moved to Keeley on the outskirts of Wootton. My father was a thatcher by trade. He died of pneumonia when I was only three years old, and mother was left to raise four children alone – I was the youngest. Father worked in Mill Hill during the summers. This was a country area at that time, and it was known as the "hay country". My sister and I both lived there later in life, and I was in Service there.

My mother earned a living making lace, and she also did pickled onions for local people, took in washing, and did all sorts of things to bring in money. My two older sisters were good, and occasionally bought me clothes to help mother out.

Each afternoon after school I used to rush home to do pillow lace with mother. She taught me how to do this when I was about eleven. My mother and other local women used to congregate in one house to make lace, and mother did this from an early age – she never went to school. May Vincent, my cousin, who lived at Keeley in what is now "Peartree Cottage", then a butcher's shop, collected the local lace and sold this to Braggins. She also selected the cottons.

On the odd occasions that I went to Bedford, I went by carrier. George Hill was the carrier, and he drove his horse and cart there on Fridays. The charge was two pence and the passengers seated themselves on the two wooden plank seats, which were on each side of the cart. George Hill lived up Keeley Lane, and his daughter, Mrs Copperwheat, who is now around ninety, still lives there.

When I was a child I used to play with my friends in the field near the Hills' property, and I was told to always come home when Emma (George's wife) lit her lamp.

Some of our favourite games were hoops, hopscotch, skipping ropes, diabolos, mothers-and-fathers, school-teachers. My childhood days were happy ones although we were poor. Grandmother lived with us in later years, before she went blind, until her death. Apart from going to church, when someone sat with grandmother, my mother never went anywhere but I never heard her complain. When father was alive he used to send her five shillings a week from Mill Hill and she thought she was well-off. He used to go up by train and stayed there with his mother who was living there at the time. I don't know what the attraction was at Mill Hill, but my brother also went there to work for a butcher at one time.'

SARAH HILLS

An Upbringing with Grandparents

'I was born in Clophill in May 1915. My parents had been living in Leighton Buzzard and my father died three months

Church Parade, Clophill, circa 1915. Miriam (Helena) was born in the room with the open window, on the left of the picture.

Miriam Hudson's aunts, Emily and Lilian, outside of the Clophill Post Office and Stores which was owned by her grandparents.

before I was born, when my mother returned to live with her parents who ran the village stores and Post Office at Clophill. Mother herself died in 1918 of 'flu, at the time of the epidemic. My grandmother (Pricilla Daniels) said that mother earned about nine shillings a week as a dressmaker, doing piece work, before she died, and had to raise four children (I had three elder brothers) on that! My grandfather (Henry Daniels) lost a hand in a sawmill accident and received compensation and this started their first business. He died in 1928. Grandmother lived to be eighty-six. She was brought up in Maulden. She went to a Dame School and later did hat work at home. Buyers came from the Luton factories to buy these hats.

When mother died my grandparents officially fostered us as this was the best way they could get financial help in bringing us up. They had periodic inspections by the Board of Guardians to ensure our welfare. There were uncles and

Henry & Priscilla Daniels, Miriam Hudson's grandparents. He died when Miriam was thirteen: Priscilla lived to be eighty-six. They held the family together.

aunts living at home, and I was thoroughly spoiled by my grandmother. We had a lot of love from all the relatives. We moved to Ampthill just before my eighth birthday, and came to live in Park Hill, near the police station. I became friendly with the Police Superintendent's daughter – and later with his son, whom I married!

When we lived at the shop there were two uncles there and one aunt, unmarried. It was always open house. Other grandchildren were always coming home. We played Ludo a lot. There were always cousins, uncles and aunts visiting: as many as eighteen met on Boxing Day for years. Our family delivered groceries and oil in the village. They kept poultry,

Miriam Hudson's family:
Betsey Dix, daughter of Luke Evans, her great great grandfather
George, her grandfather (her father's father)
John, her uncle, who had a smallholding in Maulden Road, Flitwick
Len, a signalman on the railway
Peter, who had a small-holding down Maulden Road, Flitwick.
Ebeneza, who owned sandpits at Flitwick and was Clerk to the Parish
Council
Reuben, who owned a fruit shop in Bedford, now Saxby's. The
youngest son.
Photo: C H Litchfield, Ampthill.

pigs (which grandmother sometimes fed with a bottle), rabbits
and the horse which pulled the van and was put into a trap
on Sunday for visits to the Baptist Chapel. We used to take a
huge umbrella if it rained, and walked up Flitton Hill so as
not to put a strain on the horse. This was before I turned
seven.'

HELENA 'MIRIAM' HUDSON

Living with Auntie

'I was actually born in Northamptonshire, in 1910, and following the death of my parents, came to Stagsden to live with a spinster aunt. My father was killed when he was thrown from a pony and trap in Rushden, where he was in business manufacturing shoes, and my mother died of pernicious anaemia. There had been seven children in our family, but my eldest brother died of meningitis, leaving three boys and three girls, of whom my sister Grace and I were twins. My aunt lived at Bury End which is about a mile and a half from the village, and this is the distance I walked to and from Stagsden School each day, until arrangements were made for me to enter Howard College in Bromham Road, Bedford, as a boarder.

Grace, Edith's twin sister, at the cottage at Bury End, Stagsden.

Conditions were rather primitive in Stagsden in 1922, there being no piped water supply to my aunt's cottage. Water had to be drawn from the well which was in the paddock at the side of the house, and auntie carried this on a float balanced across her shoulders. There was no sewage system either and no bathroom. Cooking was done on the range which was alight all year round. There were frequent hunts in Stagsden, which often went to ground in the woods near my aunt's home. If we were good, we were given the unfortunate fox's tail!

Stagsden was a small community, but there was a visiting baker and grocer, delivering door to door. My aunt kept hens and produced her own eggs, and milk was collected from a local farm. Auntie (Miss Thompkins) was a tailoress, and made clothes for many village people. She was a member of Bunyan Meeting Chapel in Stagsden, a Sunday School teacher, and a committed Christian. Lace-making was a popular cottage industry at that time, and I remember the lovely pillow lace which was made by Mrs Golding, who occupied a cottage belonging to Mr Newman, a local farmer. Her niece has continued the family tradition, and now teaches pillow lace-making in London.'

EDITH INKSON

A recent photograph of the cottage at Bury End.
Photo: courtesy William H Brown.

A Large Family in Bedford

'I was born in Clapham at The Folleys, in 1904 and we later moved to Bedford. There were twelve children in our family. I can remember when times were hard, when I was a boy, and the Pawn Shop was a common way of raising money. I've queued down Ram Yard for a penn'th of stale bread or cake many times. My father was a foundryman, who worked at Allens, and he was so ashamed of his rough hands that he often wore gloves. My mother used to take in soldiers' washing during the First World War, – those who were billetted locally. All this washing was done by hand, using boilers, and I recall that there was washing everywhere. My parents had moved to Castle Hill, Bedford at this time. Father was very hardworking, and used to help mother as the boys grew up, washing trousers and ironing.'

RICHARD 'TOM' LOVELL

To The Manor Born

'In 1908 my parents were living in India, where father was a Major in the Royal Field Artillery. This is where I was born. My parents had seven children of whom I was the eldest. After the First World War my parents came to live at Wootton House, [Wootton], which belonged to our family estate. Father employed domestic staff – cooks, chauffeurs, maids, gardeners, grooms, nannies and nurses and our governess – and my mother was always keen to delegate her parental responsibilities to her paid servants. The warmth, affection and attention which all children crave in childhood, I gained through my close relationship with my father. It was father who crept up to our rooms after the servants had sent us to bed. He would tuck us up and slip a little sweet under our pillow if he thought we had had a bad day.

I was taught to knit at the age of four, and have always enjoyed knitting. From the age of twelve I made clothes for my sisters, and subsequently took up dress designing.

Father treated me as a boy, and even taught me to ride a motorbike when I was fourteen. He gave me faith in my ability to do things, and this gave me confidence. I feel that I benefited greatly from this upbringing and from his influence. We always enjoyed hunting and beagling, which is the hunting of hares on foot. Father was a keen horseman and our family hunted with the Oakley and Whaddon Hunts.

A recent meet of the Oakley Hunt at The Chequers Inn, Wootton. Photo: courtesy Selena Fraser-Newstead.

I was given a car for my seventeenth birthday by my father, who was a very keen motorist and a founder member of the Bedfordshire Motor Club.'

EYVOR PELHAM REID

A Straw Hat Factory Owner's Daughter

'I was born in Luton in 1891, where my father was a straw hat manufacturer and owned his own small private factory which was built on one side of the garden. Both of my parents were Lutonians. My mother was the youngest of seven children and although she had the opportunity to go into the Post Office to work, she remained at home, to help her mother, and did not work before her marriage. She did make all of her own clothes, and was very proficient at this. Father was a lovely man. He died ten days after his fiftieth birthday, in 1915.

I had a very happy childhood indeed. I had one brother, who was three and a half years older than me. He suffered with a nervous condition and had treatment at Great Ormond Street Hospital.

I grew up in Princess Street. Several people in this street were straw hat manufacturers. I always enjoyed games, and

Dunstable Downs from Green Lane, circa 1905. Publicised as a 'healthy and bracing spot'.
Photo: courtesy Dunstable Gazette and Mr E Baldock.

my father made me a bat with which to play cricket at one time. We all used to go out walking, to Dunstable over the Downs, and returned by train, or walked to Luton Hoo and returned by train. My parents loved the countryside. My mother took a Sunday School class of over sixty children, every Sunday afternoon – and on her own. I started helping her mark the star cards for attendance when I was old enough, and after visiting to help out on one occasion, stayed for eleven years.'

HILDA PUDDEPHATT

Village Life

'I was born in Colmworth village in 1897 and the house I grew up in is still there. We had eight children in our family and I reckon that I had more illness than any of them, and yet I have outlived all the others.

My father was a tenant farmer at Rectory Farm and Church Farm. Life in the village was not at all dull. There was no electricity, television or telephone, but we used to read a lot, play the piano and go to church. I had ponies to ride and used to chase the hunters as I grew older. There were occasional visits by pony and trap, to market in Bedford and St. Neots.'

EVELINE STANTON

A Childhood Spent in Harrold

'My birthplace was the end one of three cottages which stood opposite the present garage in Harrold High Street. My father was in the leather trade, and worked in Harrold for Manton Brothers.

My mother lost her mother when she was young, and she was adopted by Charles Crawlery and his wife who kept the big hostelry, the Wheatsheaf Hotel, which took in guests. She helped in the Wheatsheaf until her marriage to my father around 1900. She always did say the vicar was drunk on that occasion, but drunk or not, he got them married! In later years everyone knew her as "nanny Thew" and she was a popular local character. She was in the habit of shopping, and continued to do so until she died, by which time she was in her nineties.

My earliest recollection is of having measles when I was three, and being taken by pushchair to see Dr Sommerville. As we passed by the corner of the Wheatsheaf – then the gathering-place of the local men, – my mother, who was quite a beauty, attracted a number of enthusiastic wolf-whistles. Another early memory is of being taken to a fete being held at the Vicarage. The vision of a bucketful of lemonade – heaven to a thirsty boy – has remained with me ever since.

When I was about seven my father took me to the pinnacle of the church to watch the London-to-Manchester air race. After waiting several hours we finally saw an aeroplane. The race was won, I believe, by a French aviator.'

In 1908 Alfred Harmsworth (Lord Northcliffe), proprietor of the Daily Mail, offered prizes for flying achievements, including £10,000 for a flight from London to Manchester. This was achieved in 1910 by a Frenchman, Louis Paulhan.

'I can remember the time when the Titanic went down, an event that few who lived at the time ever forgot.

My grandfather was a shepherd who worked for James Day at Mansion Farm. He never earned more than twelve shillings a week, never saw the sea all his life and never had a holiday, yet when he died he had £600 in gold sovereigns! He had an acre of allotment, and always kept two pigs, one of which he sold to the butcher and one he had for himself. His wife made pillow lace. There was always a sweet or a piece of ham if you went there. Being a shepherd he had to drive the sheep to market once a year and when I was ten I had to help him drive them to Bedford market, starting at four in the morning. We eventually got to Stafford Bridge, Oakley, only to find the water was in flood and the sheep wouldn't go over. We waited until a postman came and he helped grandfather

*Louis Paulhan, winner of the 1910 London to Manchester Air Race.
Photo: courtesy The Shuttleworth Collection.*

to carry one over, and then the others followed through. We came back on a horse-drawn bus, me with sweets in my pocket and three pence. After that, having developed a taste for money, I got a part-time job, 6.30am to 8.30am in Cook's bakehouse. Then 4.30pm to 6.00pm and 6.00am to 6.00pm Saturdays. For this I earned eighteen pence which was given to my mother. George Cook would give me the odd three pence on the side with a caution, "don't you say anything boy": his wife would have murdered him had she known. Mr Cook was one of the three village bakers. The villagers were almost self-sufficient, with a flour miller, two butchers, clock-maker, plumber and decorator, coal merchant, sadler, grocer, shoe maker and repairer, blacksmith, draper, baker, greengrocer, laundry, carpenter and undertaker, hurdle-maker, builder, tailor, barber and dentist, of a sort.

A shepherd at work at Bolnhurst. Photo: courtesy A Woodward.

After the First World War something arrived which affected the lives of almost everybody – the "wireless". I bought one just before Christmas 1924, and remember going up on the roof of our cottage in an attempt to get the BBC's Christmas broadcast. These were the days of the cat's whisker and earphones. The radio was an important source of information during the General Strike. Other memorable events of the postwar years included Alcock and Brown's flight across the Atlantic in 1919 and Lindbergh's single-handed crossing a few years later.

I think my mother taught me as much as the school did, morally and otherwise. She was very well-read and always bought me books when she could, and she taught me a lot about poetry. For her station in life she was one of the best-read persons, which she tried to pass on to me.

Charles Pettit, our village benefactor and the leading light in the Harrold Mutual Improvement Society (a forerunner of Adult Education classes), went on a cruise to the West Indies in 1913 with his wife, and gave a talk on his return, illustrated by lantern slides. This talk left a great impression on me because he brought back a grapefruit which he invited the audience to taste. It was the first time Harrold had seen this fruit.'

ARTHUR 'LOL' THEW

A Butcher's Son

Eric Thorne was born in Woburn in 1896, the third of five children. His father was always connected with farming cattle, sheep and pigs, as were other members of the family, living near Dunstable, Tottenhoe, Eaton Bray and Markyate, and Eric often helped these relations. At one time his father owned a butcher's shop in High Street North, Dunstable. His mother was a well educated lady who came from Warwickshire and was a nurse before she married his father.

When Eric was quite young his parents moved to Woburn House, [Beale Street], Dunstable, probably around 1902. His father bought a large piece of land there and had the house built. It was the only house at that end of the street at the time but later on others were built either side and they were owned by a relative of his father's. The rest of the land was used for farming.

'My father he worked his boys 'ard and worked his 'orses 'ard too. He said "I know I work 'em 'ard but I feed 'em well so if you feed 'em well you want to work 'em 'ard" and that's what he told people. So any rate, my eldest brother 'e sent 'im to the Grammar School and he wanted to be a soldier and at that time of the day soldiers were entertained as rubbish. You know, in a good many of these amusement halls they wouldn't have 'em in. They used to put over the amusement halls "dogs and soldiers not allowed". That's true. Of course, he went and

signed on: my father nearly went crackers. He said "that's what I spent on your education: put you in a brigade like that! But you're better there I daresay 'cos I can't do nothing with you". So anyway, he said to me when I was fourteen, "you needn't worry, I ain't wastin' no money on you". He says, "I'll make you work – I would ha' done your brother but he went to the army out o' my reach".

My father was a butcher and I remember taking meat out when I was a lad, beef tuppence a pound, and I complained about the weight – 'cos they had deep butchers' baskets then, – "you get going", he says, "donkeys go best laden" – that was the answer I got from my father. They used to charge tuppence a pound for beef and they used to give 'em a lump o' suet and you could buy the best bacon for sixpence a pound and it was cured at that time o' the day. Different to what they cure it now. At the bacon factory they electrocute them to kill them, then they go down a slide and they are not scalded now, they have these special blow pipes to burn the 'air orf and then the entrails are taken out and then they are pushed along and they spray a chemical on 'em: it won't keep the good blowflies out, it won't you know, not a chemical. Years ago they used to cure them prop'ly and you could keep bacon for days 'cos the fridges were unknown at that time o' the day.

My father he did believe in making people work. I remember once he said to me "ah", he says, "I'm short o' beef, I shall 'av to go to Hitchin market". He said "you won't be able to go to school today, you gotta come with me". So I thought it was all right, the sound of it. So he bought four of these blessed bullocks from Hitchin market, he helped me out of Hitchin and then said "there y'are, now you can get going" That's a good walk from Hitchin to Dunstable! I got to the bottom of bloomin' Offley Hill, ('cos there was no cars about), one of these bloomin' bullocks run me in a cornfield – I shall never forget it. I run no end of a time 'fore I could turn it back. At last when I did get 'em to Dunstable my father said "well you was there to stop it weren't ya".

One Christmas eve my father came 'ome in a rage: I was ten then. He says "ha", he says, "nice job: I've bin to Hornes Farm at Studham and that cow was born at the farm. Now I'm short of milk so you'll 'ave to go an' fetch her" he says. He'd got a milk round ya see. I said "what, Christmas Day?" "O' course you will, he says". Me father would knock the daylight out of me if I didn't do what I was told. So I started very early Christmas Day – six o'clock: there was a lot of snow about and there was no road there, it was only a track to Whipsnade. I never met a single soul and when I got to Hornes Farm I said to 'im "is there a cow come back here Mr Thorne bought?" He says "yeah, why?" "Well, I got to take her". "You'll never be able to take her" he says "she's born 'ere". I says "I got an 'alter in me 'and". So he put it on and it took me round the bloomin' mud 'eap. "There y'are" he says "I told ya!" Any'ow I started off and got to the crossroads. She went through the bloomin' woods, and back she went to the farm! So I went after 'er again. I said to this cowman "will you lend me an 'arrowing chain?" I says, "I'll tie it on and I'll get a bit of a branch of a tree so when she runs through the gaps I've got her then" So I arrived 'ome for my Christmas dinner at three o'clock and oh did my mother carry on. I said "'aven't you 'ad your dinner?" "No" she said "do you think I'd have it without you, 'cause I wouldn't", and she didn't half get on to my father.'

To Market to Market to Buy a Fat Pig

'I remember when I was about twelve he wanted me to go to a farm where there was a young bull and some pigs. He said "the farmer has starved the pigs and I'd like to get 'old o' some of them pigs, I'll soon get 'em fat". So when it come the day "oh" he says, "I've got a billious attack, I shalln't be able to go: you'll 'ave to go" he says. So I says "I daren't go and bid for them 'cause whatever I buy I shall buy 'em too dear". "You'll do what you're told" he says. So any rate he give me a blank cheque: "I'll tell you what to do, you stand behind two or three people so they can't see you 'cause if they know you're bidding

*for me they always run me up" he says. So some of these pigs
come in, half starved, like stags they were. I wonder they stood
up. So I bid for 'em you see. They were knocked down to me
and the auctioneer says, "who are ya?" I whispered in his ear.
So when the bull came in I bought that. I had to leave the bull
but I took the pigs 'ome in the float. So when they come out of
the bloomin' float me father says to me "crickey" he says, "I
'ope they don't die before they get out of the float".*

*He used to deal at the mill at Eaton Bray, me father did, for
years, and he had twenty ton of barley meal come in just 'fore
we 'ad these pigs and I got it all booked 'cos I thought me
father would never let me know how much money he makes on
these pigs but he will if I lose on 'em! So any rate we had these
pigs and got 'em fat and he sent 'em to Luton market and one
day when he wa'nt about I looked in his desk and I see
Cumberland's bill, the auctioneer. So I said to 'im "you made
something on them pigs all right". "'ow do you know" he said.
"'cause I know how much they ate 'cause I took particular
notice". "Ah, I wan't going to tell ya" he says "or your 'ead'll
get so big you'll never get through the door"!'*

Measuring up for Ploughman

*'My father 'ad the water turned on down the fields, and we
used to get the boys to help us water the cows. They 'ad to
carry it there with buckets and that was bloomin' 'ard work
'cos some of these cows could drink no end of water. Some of
these boys they wanted to be measured for ploughman. You
know how they measured them for ploughman? Well, when
the horse is tied up they put a box behind the horse, one fella
lifts its tail up and the other boy pushes him from behind and
then they get special diplomas wrote out. That is an old trick,
years ago when they used to measure them. Of course, kids
had to make their own fun at that time o' the day. They did.
The best of it, some of the silly beggars you know, see how
some were measured and yet they wanted to be done the same,
to get the diploma!'*

Sparrow Catching and Other Antics

'Old man Thorne who used to sell faggots in Edwards Street, [Dunstable] with blood and stuff, used to 'ave 'em on a tray. He used to sell sparrows too. They used to go round with bat folded nets into where the ivy and stuff is round the 'ouses, and get these sparrows and sell 'em at a farthing a piece. They were picked, and in a tray. They'd still 'ave their claws on. They used to catch larks on the Downs at one time.

All the boys wanted to learn to milk then. One or two boys said to me "why don't you let 'em start on the bull, they can't get the wrong teat for a start there!" We didn't mind the young ones but we'd got a big bull there a Hereford. Well, if any stranger went in he'd 'ave killed 'im. It's funny about bulls because this big Hereford bull, my brothers and I could have 'im out and we made 'im harnessed to this binder once and I put 'im in a big old farm cart and we was leading him around the field. My father had got a little trotting mare and there was a little bell on its collar and you could hear it. He'd got a rubber tyred trap, so you couldn't hear the wheels. My brother says "here comes father, I can hear him" We done our best to get this bull out this bloomin' cart but we couldn't get 'im out quick enough. Me father he nearly went mad. He said "if you ever do that again, that bull will kill ya".'

Ringing the Bull

'It's surprising, but I remember earning a gold sovereign once for ringing a bull. A man at Flamstead wanted his bull rung and he 'ad one of these big Hereford bulls and he was a fool really. You ring a bull when they're six months, and this bull was two year old and weighed about a ton. Me father said to me "you've helped me to ring bulls, would you like to earn a golden sovereign?" I said "what, would I!", 'cause I'd never handled one of them before. So on Saturday morning I went over there. My father had given me this bull ring, made of bronze metal they are, and there's a screw goes through 'em. You 'ave a long pointed knife just to sever the bull's centre piece in the nose.

*Well they snort a bit bulls do, when you do that. Any rate me
father said to me "whatever you do, don't you allow anybody to
rope this bull, do it yourself." So I went up to see this Arnold the
farmer at Flamstead and he said "well, what do you want?"
"I've come to ring your bull". He looked at me: "what, a whipper
snapper like you" he said. So I says "yes, this won't be the first
one I've rung." I says "I know he's a big one by his age". "He
weighs a ton" he says. The cowman was there and he says "I'll
tell you what I'll do for you, I'll rope him then you can do the
rest". I says "no, I shalln't do that, my father says I've got to rope
him" So he says "don't you think I know how to rope a bull,
haven't I had more experience than you?" I says "yes, I bet you
know how to do it better, but if you happen to forget one of these
knots and it gets loose and I'm in there", I says "I'm finished". So
I roped him and I rung 'im and I got me golden sovereign and
the old lad said "you've made a good job of it" When I went
home, me father said on the quiet "did Arnold pay you?" "Yes" I
says. One day I fetched this golden sovereign out of me pocket
and me mother spotted it. She says "where did you get that
from?" I says "I done a little job". "A little job" she says, "you
don't get golden sovereigns for doing little jobs". She says to me
father "where did he get it from?" He says "he earned it". And me
father told her. "I should think you want to put me up the
cemetery. If anything had gone wrong he'd have killed me" she
said, "don't you ever do anything like that again."*

*It's all right when they're young, but if anybody knows what
they're doing, if you rope an animal prop'ly it's impossible for
them to get away, it is, unless the ropes break. But you don't
put an old rope on a big bull, you don't take chances. Nobody
does in their right mind. You see, you get the ropes over the
back from the front leg and also the back leg and you rope 'em
so if they move one leg it pulls the other one, so it's impossible
for them to get into action. They couldn't turn round quick and
charge you, 'cause if they did, well they'd smash you you see.
And when you get the ropes on and get them tied up you want
a long pointed knife and then you just pierce the centre piece,*

put the ring through and then put the little screw on. They don't move 'cause you rope 'em so they cannot. So when I released the rope I waited 'til he shook them clear and pulled them from under the door. I never 'ad any trouble but I would 'av done if I'd gone in there afterwards! You'd got to do that for even at that time of the day the penalty for taking a bull through the streets was £500. If any man took a bull over six months even if it was amongst cows, they were liable for a £500 penalty. If they once got put out they could do untold damage, these bulls, but if they are rung, they can't, because you see what you do, you have a rope from the bull's horns, and just through it's ring and turn it once and you can lead it like an old goat. That's its nerve centre. You can do anything with a bull like that; even if they was to charge, if they'd got a rope on their 'ead you could get hold of that and steady them and lead them about like a goat. That's why the penalty was so great; they wouldn't allow people to take bulls through the street unless they were roped. Some people preferred to lead them on a long pole rather than a rope. The people that used the poles were people that was a bit nervous, in case the bull might turn quick, but it didn't matter, I didn't think much of the poles me-self. Even in these cattle shows they used to use them'

Winners and Losers

'They used to 'ave a grand Christmas market at Leighton and there was a nearby farmer – he used to win no end of prizes. He was a bright specimen he was. He won no end of money with his cattle and if you'll believe me, he got caught travelling from Luton to St. Pancras once with a season ticket that was twelve months old. He'd been travelling backwards and forwards for twelve months on this old ticket. He didn't half cop it for that job. But I never thought you 'ad people round Leighton that'd do a thing like tha'.

We 'ad to work 'ard for the money we got and when I earned myself a golden sovereign I kidded myself on I was a millionnaire. I'd never 'ad a golden sovereign before. They were in circulation at that time of the day.'   ERIC THORNE

95

Hard Times in Thurleigh Village

'I was actually born in Ilford, Essex and christened John, but always called "Jack". My father was a monumental mason and he was killed in a road accident whilst cycling to work up Barnet Hill. He was knocked off his bicycle by horses that shied and ran him down. That was in February of 1911. There were four children in our family and the fourth was born after my father died. I was the second child. 1911 was the first year in which compensation was paid under the Compensation Act, the Old Age Pension and National Insurance Act, 1911. Even so, mother had very little money, and returned to Cross End, Thurleigh, her birth place, to be near her parents. Ours was the poorest family in the village then.

There was no local transport at the time and my mother bought a pony and provided a service taking people to the local station. She also provided transport for occasional weddings. She kept chickens and a cow at one time.

I left school at thirteen to work on the land, but I was driving horses on the farm when I was as young as nine. The shire horses were very kind, they knew more than I did. I just walked beside them. We lived next to a farm, so all of my leisure time was spent on the farm. There were all kinds of animals and all kinds of crops on the farm. The crops were rotated – wheat, beans, oats, clover, barley – over a seven-year period. Wheat beans, wheat again, winter oats, clover, wheat, and fallow the next year. As children we found plenty to do, rabbit hunting, riding on the empty cart and walking back with it when it was full, during harvesting. It was great fun. Sundays we always attended Sunday School and church. Mother was a Christian woman who always kept the Sabbath for rest and worship. She would never allow us to sing on a Sunday, except in worship, and games were strictly forbidden.'

JOHN 'JACK' THORNE

The Village Bobby's Daughter

'I was born in Bassingbourne, Cambridge, which is near Royston, where my father was a police constable. In later years I came to live in Maulden.

Bassingbourn-cum-Kneesworth (near Royston) circa 1905. A farming community. Front right is Hitcock's Grocery & Drapery, next the Whitbey Public House, and in the distance the birthplace of Gladys Wallis (neé Frost). Photo: courtesy Cambridgeshire Collection, Cambridgeshire Libraries.

My father left school at nine years of age and worked on a farm to help the family finances. He was one of twelve or thirteen children. I can remember twelve of them and his mother. I never remember seeing her walking about and the father had died long before my time. I have been told that he was a Methodist preacher who visited surrounding villages – on foot. I have heard my father talk of driving geese to market a distance of eight miles or more, and being rewarded with a few pence. It was a long walk for a boy of about twelve but I think he got a lift home in a farm cart. He joined the Cambridgeshire Police Force and met my mother when he was stationed at the little town of Soham in the Fen Country not far from Ely. They married in 1903 and went to the little village of Bassingbourne near Royston, where they lived until 1915.

My father was a great country lover and he knew all the country lanes where the wild honeysuckle grew. One of my earliest childhood memories is of coming down in the morning to find a large bowl of wild honeysuckle on the living room table. It was so delightfully scented. Another happy memory is of going "nutting" with him in the woods near the village where he spent his boyhood.

A picture of The Knoll, Maulden, taken before the first world war. Photo: courtesty Mrs B Keens.

I have spent over sixty years in Maulden. Mr Percy Giles was the first village postmaster I knew. Transport used by the post office now differs greatly from the high horse-drawn box mail-carts which I recall from my childhood. They were painted bright red with the royal cipher painted on them. I remember the mail-man in our village well and can visualise him hunched up and wrapped up on the mail-cart with his horse clip-clopping along. He had no real protection whatever from the weather.

Mr Giles also sold grocery and some drapery. There were bales of white and unbleached calico, and flannelette on shelves at one side. Sugar, butter and tea were weighed out as required. Biscuits were loose in tins stacked in front of the counter and they too were weighed out as required. Few if any sweets were wrapped but were kept in large glass jars. Very pretty they looked too. If they stuck together in the jars they were loosened with a steel (used for sharpening knives) or a knife. Bacon was sliced and weighed as required. Paraffin oil could be bought for about tenpence a gallon. Later on it was delivered to the door by a Flitwick man and for years cost elevenpence per gallon. People relied on it for cooking and heating and lighting. Accounts of purchases were kept in small books in which orders were recorded and there was a Christmas bonus based on the amount of each person's purchases.

Milk has always been delivered daily in my time here. I believe it was at one time delivered twice daily but that would have been before the days of refrigerators and milk marketing boards. It was served from can to jug in half-pint or one-pint measures as required. It was before the time of pasteurisation too and had to be boiled, if kept overnight. Ugh!!

Meat supplies were delivered daily except for Mondays. (Families finished up the cold Sunday joints on Mondays.) A good joint cost five shillings to seven and sixpence. Mr Charles Summerfield delivered meat for Tansley's butchers' shop in Woburn Street. Everitts' men brought meat round on carrier bicycles with large compartments for meat in baskets on the front.

Coal was delivered in one hundredweight bags. Our coalman was Mr Teddy Burgoine who used a horse and cart for delivery. Mr Burgoine's daughter still lives in the village. She tells me that one pound per ton was quite a usual price for coal in her father's time. Each cottager received a free bag of coal at Christmas time, I presume through one of the Maulden Charities. It was very welcome in those days of low wages, and big families.

I clearly remember the death of Edward VII in 1910. I went to call for my special playmate at a farm near where we lived. Lying in their porch was their morning paper with great black headlines. "The King Dies: Queen Alexandra is prostrate with grief". I had never encountered the word "prostrate" before and it was some time before I knew the meaning of it. I pictured the poor queen lying down unable to move!

I was playing "mud pies" with my special playmate when I saw my very first aeroplane. For a very long time after that everybody ran out to look if an aeroplane passed overhead.

I recall Coronation Day, June 22 1911, when King George V and Queen Mary were crowned. I would have been nearly seven years old. The thing that I most vividly remember is being presented with my very first silver sixpence by the girl who used to wheel me out in my pram when I was a baby. She had been away in domestic service and had returned to her home village for the Coronation celebrations. I remember that it was in the field where the Coronation celebrations were held that I found my first "bee archis", a little flower very aptly named.'

GLADYS WALLIS

Life in Haynes

'I was born in Hounslow, Middlesex in 1906. My father was Haynes born, and this is where all his family lived. His mother kept a little grocery shop opposite the Greyhound public house in Northwood End. My mother was born in Wiltshire and had been in service in Hounslow and this is where she met my father, who was working as a builder's labourer, (a yardman) in Chiswick at the time. When he was called up into the army in 1914 my mother moved back to

Haynes to be near his family. They had six children, three girls and three boys.

Father was killed in action on 4 November 1918,and armistice was signed on 11 November. My youngest brother was born on 23 November of that year. Times were difficult for mother but she managed somehow. She'd often boil up half a pig's head, and pork rinds, and made lovely brawn. We always had a good breakfast of porridge, and although she would "get by" during the week, she always produced a good meal for Sunday lunch. We children were happy enough. Easter was a time for collecting primroses, which could be sold in the market. Journeys to Bedford meant walking to Southall Station and getting the train, but it was fun for us children. There was plenty to do in the country, never a dull moment.

The village playing fields used to be farmland. I've done quite a lot of farm work, picking runner beans, peasing, potato picking and helping with threshing at harvest time. The sheaths were stood in the field until dry, then stacked until the threshing engine came to thresh the corn.'

BEATRICE 'MAY' WEBB

Childhood in Stagden Village

I was born in Stagsden West End in 1907, in my father's small tied cottage. At that time all Bedfordshire was agricultural. Father was horse keeper firstly to Mr Henman and then to the subsequent landowner of West End Farm, Mr Ben Howkins. There were eleven children in our family, eight of whom were born in this cottage. This is situated about two miles out of the village.

Whilst I was a boy there was a diptheria epidemic in the area but it didn't touch our family. Then followed scarlet fever. Four of us children were taken to Clapham Isolation Hospital, where it was usual to remain for six weeks. I was kept in for seven weeks and my sister for twelve weeks. My

Horace's mother outside her cottage in Spring Lane, Stagsden.
Thought to have been taken in the early 1950s. She died in 1958.

Horace Welch's father, photographed in 1919, proudly displaying a
horse which he bred for his employer, Mr Howkins, West End
Farm, Stagsden. The farmhouse is in the background.

father came to visit twice as I recall. The hospital was six or seven miles away from our home. My older sisters visited on Saturdays and Wednesdays on their bicycles. The hospital meals were very monotonous: bread and butter and bread and dripping. For dinner potatoes, meat and haricot beans. Eggs were only available if parents sent them. Fruit or sweets also had to be sent in. There used to be one doctor serving three or four parishes in those days – Stagsden, Turvey, Stevington. In 1911 National Insurance started but it only covered the payer, not his wife and children, so people had a 'doctor's club'. This was twelve and a half pence per quarter, rising to approximately twenty-five pence.

Horace Welch's parents' diamond wedding celebrations, with all their relations, pictured in the Stagsden School Yard.

In our village, tradesmen called on their rounds, bakers each day, butcher twice weekly. Everything was brought to the door. People only went to Bedford for clothes, but a draper also came round, taking orders. A lot of traders came from

Mother's cottage today. Now derelict, the lattice windows have dropped from their frames.

Cranfield too. In the village there were three shops – general stores, sweets and tobacco, etc. All villages had a blacksmith, and the Stagsden blacksmith is still in business. There were three pubs, a cobler (two or three people did shoe repairs), there was someone who mended watches, repaired bicycles, and sold honey and things from his allotments. Everything one needed could be had in the village. The carrier's cart went from North Crawley in Buckinghamshire, to Bedford, calling at Stagsden between 9 and 10 am and returning about four in the afternoon. Once a year the children in our family were taken to Bedford and visited a teashop there. This was a real treat. The carrier's cart was open-topped. This continued to offer transportation until after the First World War, when the buses started. My mother would only use the carrier's cart while it still operated.'

HORACE WELCH

Enjoyment of the Outdoors

'When I was younger we lived at the top of High Town Road. Luton was more of a country place then. From where we lived, at the top of High Town Road, you could just go up the hill to Stopsley and walk across to the villages then. My stepmother was very kind and we had a lady visit us from Cockenhoe who had many boys for whom mother made clothes, as she was very good at dress-making. This lady walked from Cockenhoe through Round Green, and called in for a cup of tea before going to do her shopping in town. She'd then call back for the things mother made for her. I used to walk her part of the way home. It was all countrified along by Stopsley High School, but things have to change, I accept that. There is no use arguing.

We have always enjoyed the outdoor life. When I was young we often used to go to Nomansland, taking the train to Wheathampstead. We'd go for the day, and walk from the station through the village and over the hill to the common. It was a popular place, for picnics, cricket and so on.'

ETHEL MAYES

SCHOOLDAYS

SCHOOLDAYS

Introduction

Since the eighteenth century various establishments have existed for the education of a minority of children, such as the Charity School, Sunday School, Ragged School, Dame School, Grammar School and Public School. It was not until 1867 when thousands of working men were given the vote, that educational provision came to be regarded as important from a political viewpoint, and shortly after, in 1870, the Forster's Act evolved a country-wide plan for educating the masses. School Boards were then created, to deal with provision for children aged five to twelve years. In 1876 education became compulsory. Management of schools eventually became the responsibility of local authorities when the Balfours Act of 1902 was passed. The school meals service began in 1906 and from 1907 scholarships became available allowing some children of poor families, the opportunity to attend Grammar Schools. At the turn of the century the school leaving age was fourteen, but during the First World War children were permitted to leave at an earlier age as an aid to the war effort, to work on the land.

After the 1870 Act new schools began to appear in villages and towns, often labelled 'School Board'. The advent of compulsory education meant that all children aged from five to thirteen years, untutored and unaccustomed to the regime and rigours of school life, were suddenly obliged to attend local schools. It is not difficult to imagine the chaotic state of these early schools, struggling to maintain order and discipline, and to implement programmes of teaching in times of grave shortages of teachers. There were naturally children who found the rigours of school too much, and those whose parents were not so supportive of the education system, not having been a part of it themselves. The suspension or expulsion of problem children must have seemed an attractive option to teachers of the day. Parents struggling to make a living understandably resented the loss of a potential wage earner in the older children, especially boys. It has been suggested that the high walls or spiked iron railings which surrounded many schools were designed for the purpose of keeping parents out and children in!

The School Boards were abolished following the Balfour Eduction Act of 1902, and from September 1903 local authorities became responsible for running schools. How interesting to note that after so many years, many local authorities have recently been forced to relinquish such responsibility.

Each village and each district had its own community school, and the children were no strangers to each other, since all lived locally to the school, within walking distance. Separate entrances to the schools were common in Victorian times, entrances set well apart and marked Boys and Girls. The entrances normally led into the cloakroom areas and thence into the classroom. Toilet 'blocks' were often to be found across the playground, or situated externally to the main building. Stone floored and tiled corridors, polished wood floors in schoolrooms, painted internal brickwork, glazed and panelled interior dividers, high beamed ceilings, high-set windows. Dimly lit and chilly in winter-time, these early schools certainly possessed character. Solid structures standing resolute, built to endure, as would the system itself.

'I started school at the age of three, in Milton Ernest, and used to walk there with my brothers and sisters. The bell in the turret summoned the children to school each day. This

Stagsden School and School House.

Sitting to attention! Britain Street School, Dunstable, (now known as Priory School) circa 1915.

was a Victorian Church of England school. Lighting was by oil lamp and heating was provided by one coal fire in each room. It could be very cold in winter and I've known children to cry with cold hands and feet. The rooms were quite dark and the windows so high you could not see out of them.'

WALTER 'REG' PARROTT

Many of the sturdy Victorian school buildings remain to this day, some still operating as schools. Others have been sold and converted for residential use, or used for commercial purposes. Such schools look most attractive, built of brick or stone, often with stone mullioned windows, decorated facia and hand-crafted tiled roofs.

School rooms were furnished with solid oak rows of iron-framed desks, fronting onto the master's pedestal, with little more than a blackboard as a teaching aid. Children sat to attention as lessons proceeded. Heating was inadequate in very severe wintery conditions, with open fires serving large

Northwood End School, Haynes, now converted to a private dwelling. Photo: courtesy Mr A Hutchinson.

Livingstone School, Bedford.

classrooms. Children, seated passively on benches, are known to have been so cold on occasions as to be reduced to tears.

'I was obliged to complain to the caretaker yesterday morning. The fires at 9 o'clock had the appearance of having just been lighted. Teachers had in some classes to add bundles of chips. The temperature of most rooms was about freezing point.'

(FROM THE HEADMASTER'S LOG,
HARPUR TRUST BOYS ELEMENTARY SCHOOL,
BEDFORD, 4 DECEMBER 1916.)
COURTESY: COUNTY RECORDS OFFICE

Open fires, and the Tortoise stoves later introduced, heated only a small area, with heat loss due to high ceilings and solid brick walls. High windows are another feature of Victorian schools – highly placed to minimise the risk of distraction to pupils!

By the turn of the century the system was well established and a second generation had commenced schooling. There was so much to learn, and many of these young people were eager pupils. Lessons often took a practical form and country children found 'gardening' and 'nature walks' exciting and meaningful.

With few resources, those teachers who had imagination motivated children to learn of things of which the children had no prior knowledge. School offered an opportunity to expand their horizons and – prior to the advent of radio, television and motorised transport – when life was very insular, gave young people access to knowledge which would otherwise have been denied them. Country affairs proceeded uninterrupted, in seasonal regularity, and the extraneous might well have seemed irrelevant, but with limited resources, educators could still arouse enthusiasm and excitement in children. Reading, Writing and Arithmetic, together with Religion and Christian philosophies, provided the basic curriculum, but there is no doubt that skills, knowledge and understanding extended into other undefined areas under the leadership of enthusiastic and dedicated teachers of the day.

Teachers in Training

In an effort to supply trained and competent teachers to teach in the many schools brought into being following the introduction of compulsory elementary education, a system of licensing teachers was commenced.

Young people who showed ability in school could be selected for training as firstly Monitors, for a year, and then as Pupil-teachers for a further period of four years. Pupil-teachers assisted in the teaching task, under the direction of the Headteacher or Governess, who would deal with misconduct among pupils, and allow the pupil-teacher to assist with lesson-preparation (e.g. blackboard sketches) – in consultation. The Headteacher would explain what was to be done and how to do it. It was usual for the trainee to be paid 2/6d per week, increasing to about 12/- a week (circa 1912–1917). The pupil-teacher would normally commence with the teaching of younger children, gradually progressing to the middle rooms and the older children. The Headteacher had the task of instructing the trainee teacher in teaching theory and practice. In essence, this was a form of apprenticeship. This system of teacher training actually began in the mid 19th century, was expanded in the 1870s and continued until the end of the century – later in some counties. Initially the training of elementary school teachers replaced the discredited monitorial system, and the novice was trained only to a standard which would enable him or her to teach at an elementary level.

This form of teacher training commenced at the age of thirteen and continued for five years, when at eighteen the trainee could sit an examination for the Queen's Scholarship, and enter a teacher training college. A government grant was available. Various centres emerged, offering tuition to pupil-teachers from different schools, which was regarded as a superior method of training than the purely in-house training previously conducted by each school. Trainee teachers were required to attend Saturday classes, in order to prepare for subject examinations. Pupil-teachers could continue their 'apprenticeship' and part-time studies and qualify without going to college full-time.

After 1884 the starting age for pupil-teachers was raised, and when secondary schooling became available, the pupil-teacher system of access to the profession ceased to exist, but in some areas the system persisted until well into the 20th century.

Under the 1921 Education Act, conditions for recognition of Certificated and Uncertificated Teachers were defined as follows:

Bedfordshire County Council.

EDUCATION COMMITTEE.

TELEPHONE Nº 134. 501.

H E BAINES
DIRECTOR OF EDUCATION

B/B/E.

SHIRE HALL,
BEDFORD.

19th December 192 3.

Dear Sir,

Scholarships for Monitors and Monitresses.

I am directed to inform you that the Education Committee have awarded a Scholarship to your daughter, Constance Sanders. The Scholarship, which is tenable at the Saturday Classes for Teachers held at Bedford, consists of

1. The value of the tuition fees.
2. The use of the necessary books.
3. Payment of approved travelling expenses.

The Scholarship will enable your daughter to prepare for the Preliminary Certificate Examination of the Board of Education and will terminate in December, 1926, unless she has previously passed an Examination which will qualify her as an Uncertificated Teacher, in which case the Scholarship will be terminated earlier. The Scholarship may be withdrawn at any time if your daughter's conduct, progress or health is unsatisfactory.

The Elementary Education Sub-Committee have decided to recommend the Education Committee to appoint her as a Monitress at Wootton Council Mixed School, and she should take up her duties there on 8th January, the day on which the school re-opens after the Christmas Holidays.

In view of the fact that she is a Scholarship holder and will be attending the Teacher Training Classes in Bedford on Saturdays, your daughter is entitled to absent herself from school two half-days or one whole day each week. She should consult the Head Teacher of the school in order that a convenient day, or days, may be fixed for this purpose.

Kindly inform me not later than Saturday, 22nd instant, whether you wish to accept the Scholarship on behalf of your daughter on these terms; if so, she should attend at the Council School, Queen's Park, Bedford, on Saturday, 12th January, 1924, at 9 a.m.

I am,
Yours faithfully,
HE Baines
Director of Education.

Mr. Sanders,
High Street,
Wootton,
Bedford.

Constance Sanders, (Connie Robinson), Monitoress, wins a scholarship, 1923. The first step towards becoming a teacher.

SCHEDULE 1
RECOGNITION OF TEACHERS (Article 1)

Certificated Teachers
1.   In order to obtain recognition as a Certificated Teacher a person must satisfy the Board of his health and physical capacity for teaching, and must –
(a) complete an approved Course in a Training College and pass an approved Final Examination; or
(b) pass an approved Final Examination for a University Degree and complete an approved course of training in the principles and practice of teaching; or
(c) pass an approved Final Examination for a University Degree, complete four years' approved teaching service and obtain an approved Teaching Diploma awarded by a university; or
(d) be recognised by the Scottish Education Department as a Certificated Teacher or by the Board, under arrangements made with any Government in His Majesty's dominions for the mutual recognition of teaching qualifications, as having a status corresponding to that of a Certificated Teacher; or
(e) possess such other qualifications as the Board consider substantially equivalent to the ordinary qualifications and are prepared to approve having regard to the available supply of Certificated Teachers and candidates.

Uncertificated Teachers
2.   In order to obtain recognition as an Uncertificated Teacher a person must be over 18 years of age, must satisfy the Board of his health and physical capacity for teaching, and must –
(a) pass an examination approved as a First or Second Examination for Secondary School purposes; or
(b) pass an approved Final Examination for a University Degree; or
(c) possess such other qualifications as the Board consider substantially equivalent to the ordinary qualifications and are prepared to approve having regard to the available supply of Uncertificated Teachers and candidates.

Education Act 1921
Grant Regulations No. 8 (1926)
STATUTORY RULES AND ORDERS
1926 No. 856

Courtesy: County Records Office

Teachers Reminisce

'I started in the Infants at Chapel Street School in Luton, and transferred at seven to the Dunstable Road School, a new school at the time, [opened 1898], with a lovely Headmaster called Mr Needham [a Headteacher at four Luton schools for forty-five years]. I was very happy at school and from Dunstable Road transferred to Luton's first Grammar School on Park Square, when I was about twelve. It stood on the site of the present Technical College. I remained there until I was seventeen.

The Headmaster was a Cambridge Wrangler, [TAE Sanderson, who had previously taught at military college], a mathematician. Maths was not my best subject by a very long way. Miss Gardener was my teacher of English and German, a very nice Victorian-type lady. The curriculum included French and German, but not Latin. I don't remember being encouraged to enter the teaching profession, but several of the girls in the same form as I took up teaching. My first teaching post was at the Church School in Buxton Road, Luton, in 1909.

In those days those wishing to enter the teaching profession did not attend college. We used to go to Bedford one day a week for 'method' and that sort of thing. The Method Mistress came once a month to hear us give a 'Criticism Lesson'. We really trained with experience: we had to give lessons for the Headmistress, you know, during the week. For the Criticism Lesson the Headmistress would listen to your lesson and would say something about it. The Method Mistress would write her criticism in a book, a sort of Log of the trainee's development. My first Criticism Lesson at Buxton Road Church School in Luton [opened 1874] was with five year olds. This was on the subject of the orange. We had to give these "object" lessons. I can remember one criticism, when she said "you forgot to mention the pungent smell"!

The children sat on the gallery, not in nice chairs with tables. Wooden seats, different tiers, going up and up, with a sort of bench in front. They had slates and pencils to begin with. I cannot remember any decoration of classrooms. There were only two classes in the big room, with a curtain between, and this led out to the room for the five year olds.

When I came to Surrey Street, Luton, [opened in 1891], around 1911, I did most of my teaching with infants, aged five to seven. At that time the Headmistress hadn't got a room. She sat at a table in one of the big classrooms. She would be there when you gave a lesson, if you had the class at that end. The staff had no room at all. One Headmistress had a table in the store room.The lavatories were right across the playground, very old-fashioned ones. The end one was kept locked for the staff. Wooden seats – very primitive.

I have seen some changes in my time. The children were taught basics in those days, such as their tables. The infants would learn to count in tens up to a hundred, and in fives, and they would know the composition of number ten, because it would help with their addition and subtraction. They didn't

Music and movement for pupils of Surrey Street Infants School, Luton, in the Headmistress's garden. Photo: courtesy Luton News.

find it boring – and we had classes of fifty. In fact I can remember in the war, having just over fifty in the reception class, with all the refugees. In those days the mothers were at home, doing their work at home. My father's machinists who machined the straw hats, had the machines in their own homes. They were there with their children and the children were trained properly. We did not have these unruly children like they do today.

I was very happy in Buxton Road – lovely children and such a nice Headmistress. I was fortunate in having such nice helpful people when I began teaching. With regard to the reading, under one Headmistress we made a lot of our own apparatus out of wood, when we were teaching the long sound: we made the hessian bags to put them in. I made a lot of apparatus later on when we were doing the visual method. The children would be shown whole words related to pictures and I always introduced a new word with a question, perhaps, or something which would create interest in the child. For instance, when introducing the word 'mother' I had a picture and would say "there is somebody who loves you very much". "Mummy" they would say, you see. I would say "yes, you call her mummy but she has got another name: I wonder what that is, which I should say – do you know what it is?" They would all listen and think. Someone would give me the answer and I would say "yes, 'mother', there is the picture of mother, now you go and hang the word 'mother' against the picture of mother". I can remember the word 'look'. I would say – holding my hands up – "there are two big eyes looking at you, and that word says "look". When they had learned a number of words I would spread them out on the table and ask someone to come and find 'mother', or 'boat', or whatever, and they would pick it up. I would arrange it so that the words I asked for would make a sentence. The child would hold up the word they had said and I would arrange them in the correct order and get somebody in the class to read this sentence from the children.

Then they were taught the phonic method as well. One Christmas holiday I went for a course to Keble College, Oxford, on Reading, and one important thing I have never forgotten. Dr Cyril Burt said "there are two types of children, the visualisers and those who do it with sound. Therefore you must take both methods", which we did. We started with the visual which was more interesting for the children to begin with, and then we taught the sounds and the phonograms, where they had to know those, and that is where we made a lot of our own apparatus for the children in the reception class. We had the Janet and John system in Reception, and they could read a little book by the end of term. I had a reading corner where they could go and pick up the different things they had learned, and read. We used to have a period at the beginning of the morning where the children could choose what to do – play with sand, go in the reading corner, Wendy House, or play shops. Others would sit and build with little bricks.

In earlier days there was less variety and little opportunity for choosing for themselves. They had little wooden cases at Buxton Road, with wooden cubes in and every child had the same. They were limited when sitting in the gallery; they couldn't have a lot of things about. This must have been more monotonous for them. But I never had the feeling that they were bored and needed coercion. We had no unruly children – mischievous perhaps but you could soon right them. We had exercises in the playground in early times but there was not a lot of movement. They did not move about like they do today, or as in the latter part of my teaching. School outings were very rare, but we did take them to Luton Hoo occasionally. The great thing children needed, and they do today, is encouragement. A lot of them want encouragement. I am thinking of the infants especially.

I retired in 1957, [after approximately forty-six years at Surrey Street Infants School] when I was sixty-five years old. I was Deputy Head in the last few years, but had no desire ever to be a Head as I loved the teaching. I didn't want the administrative side of the job. My favourite subject was reading. The children could read in those early days. Why there are teenagers who are illiterate now I cannot understand. Well, I can understand in some ways because it's the silly trendy methods which some of them have had.

Miss Puddephatt's retirement celebration, Surrey Street Infants School, Luton, 1957. Photo: courtesy Luton News.

We were student teachers for a year when I began teaching, and my first salary was £40 a year. Summer holiday was a month, in August, and then there was a week at Christmas. A week at Easter, I believe. Change was a matter of natural progression then, according to the headmistress and her ideals, there were no government schemes. Infant education was unchanged basically. Some children did better when we had Grammar Schools. Those who were good enough to go on to a Grammar School needed stretching and the others

Miss Puddephatt's farewell speech.
Left to right: Dr Corbett, Director of Education, Miss Edith Currant,
former Headmistress, Alderman Sir John Burgoyne, Mayor
(1938–1943) and Chairman of Luton Education Committee (1938
until, with a short break, 1953), Mr Lesley Bowles, Mayor of Luton
and Chairman of the Education Committee, Mrs Henderson,
Headmistress. Photo: courtest Luton News.

needed encouragement and practical work. The Secondary
Modern gave them an opportunity to get to the top, unlike the
Comprehensives, which they have now. People talk about
equality, but we are not all equal. They can all have equality
of opportunity though in their own age groups, but in
the different schools they can take on different things. I
believe some children want to do more practical work.

I think one of the great mistakes today with the
Comprehensive schools is that they are far too big. The staff
do not know each other where there are so many on the staff,
and the Headmaster doesn't know a child by looking in a file:

you know the children by being with them. They are not supervised in the same way as they used to be.'

HILDA PUDDEPHATT

An open evening and display of the children's best handwriting and craft work, at Surrey Street Infants School, Luton. Circa 1930.

'I left school when I was fourteen. I took the Pupil-teacher examination at the Town Hall in Bedford and having passed this, went on to attend Queens Park School on Saturdays for instruction in my specialist subjects, – whilst teaching. This continued for three years and was followed by a final examination which lasted for one week. I passed with Honours in music and arithmetic and so became an 'uncertificated teacher'. I then taught on 'supply' for twelve months at Dunstable, Dean, Keysoe, Eastcotts, Cranfield and Marston and after this 'apprenticeship' period, I applied for a vacancy at Wootton Primary School and was accepted. I have since taught at the Infant Schools in Bedford Road, Wootton –

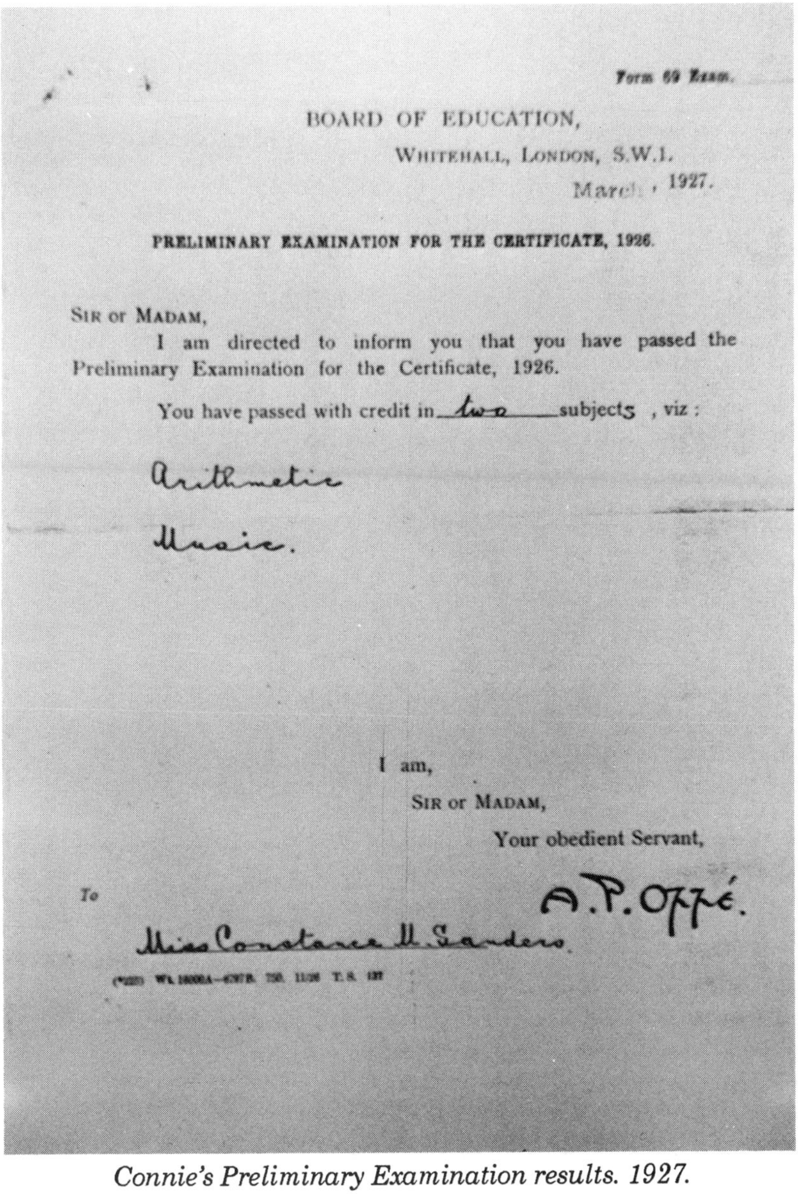

Form 69 Exam.

BOARD OF EDUCATION,

WHITEHALL, LONDON, S.W.1.

March, 1927.

PRELIMINARY EXAMINATION FOR THE CERTIFICATE, 1926.

SIR or MADAM,

I am directed to inform you that you have passed the Preliminary Examination for the Certificate, 1926.

You have passed with credit in *two* subjects , viz :

Arithmetic

Music.

I am,

SIR or MADAM,

Your obedient Servant,

A.P. Oppé.

To

Miss Constance M. Sanders.

Connie's Preliminary Examination results. 1927.

125

All communications should be addressed to—
"The Secretary."

Form 80E.

BOARD OF EDUCATION,

WHITEHALL, LONDON, S.W.1.

31st January, 1928.

Please write
at the head of
any further
communication
on this subject: | Full Name of Teacher   Sanders, Constance Marie

Reference No. P. 28/675 W/1

The Board of Education hereby notify you that you are qualified for recognition as an Uncertificated Teacher under Schedule I. 2 of the Code of Regulations for Public Elementary Schools from 3rd January, 1928 subject to your satisfying the Board as to your age and as to your health and physical capacity for teaching, in accordance with the directions given in the enclosed Rules 39.

In order that the Board may be in a position to issue your Service Book to the Local Education Authority at an early date it is particularly requested that the required evidence may be forwarded with as little delay as possible. It would be of assistance to the Board if it could reach this Office within two weeks from the date of this notification.

Form 1045 C.R.

To Miss C. M. Sanders,
Council School,
Keysoe,
St. Neots,
Huntingdonshire.

(799) Wt.16848—2283. 14,000. 11/27. T.S. 177

Connie qualifies as an Uncertificated Teacher. 1928.

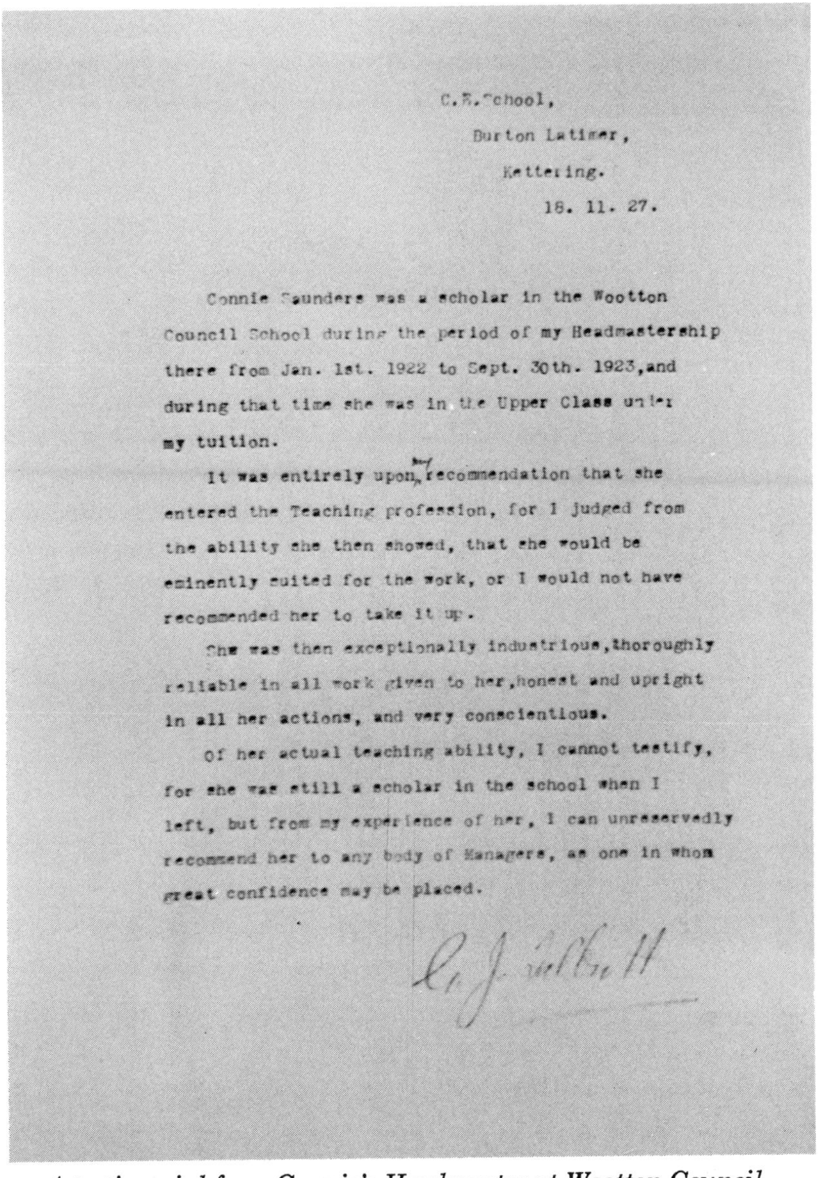

C.E.School,

Burton Latimer,

Kettering.

16. 11. 27.

Connie Saunders was a scholar in the Wootton Council School during the period of my Headmastership there from Jan. 1st. 1922 to Sept. 30th. 1923,and during that time she was in the Upper Class under my tuition.

It was entirely upon my recommendation that she entered the Teaching profession, for I judged from the ability she then showed, that she would be eminently suited for the work, or I would not have recommended her to take it up.

She was then exceptionally industrious,thoroughly reliable in all work given to her,honest and upright in all her actions, and very conscientious.

Of her actual teaching ability, I cannot testify, for she was still a scholar in the school when I left, but from my experience of her, I can unreservedly recommend her to any body of Managers, as one in whom great confidence may be placed.

A testimonial from Connie's Headmaster at Wootton Council School. It was he who encouraged her to enter the teaching profession.

the original and the present school, after the original school was demolished. I have taught privately too, for Angela and Quentin Crewe the playwright and author, when they lived at Wootton House. I taught their daughter, Candida, now a journalist, before she became a pupil at Kensington High School.

I myself was a pupil at the Infant School (the Church School) and Wootton Primary School, when Mr and Mrs Talbutt were the Heads, and occupied the school house attached to the school. A later Headmaster was Mr Meppam, whose name has now been given to a road in the village.

Inside the Victorian school the Main Hall was divided by curtains and there was also a room which was partitioned but which could be opened up to enlarge the hall. There was one other room attached. It was very crowded, and lessons were not very exciting in my day. Children were seated at long desks with iron-framed seats attached. There were pens, pencils, ink wells, slates and slate pencils – not much to fire a child's imagination. Five to six children sat at each desk, and if anyone needed to leave their seat, then all the others had to stand to let him or her out. There was little movement in fact. The girls wore starched pinafores with a handkerchief pinned to the front.

Many children had to walk to school from the Stewartby area and Bourne End. Lunches were not provided then, and the children each brought their own food. You could buy a cup of cocoa at school for the princely sum of 2d per week.'

CONSTANCE ROBINSON

It is just sixty-six years since I left school to take up my first teaching post. A great friend of mine had held the post and it was offered to me when she died tragically at the age of nineteen. It was in the era of slates and slate-pencils and I can still hear the awful squeak of pencil on slate which set one's teeth on edge. But the more mischievous boys enjoyed competition with one another.

Mr Morris came into my classroom one day. Among other questions he asked me if the heating was efficient. As the room was very large and very high and the only heating was from a large double Kitchener stove at one end I gave him a truthful answer. I told him we roasted at one end of the room and froze at the other. I got a gentle ticking off from the headmaster for being indiscreet.'

GLADYS WALLIS

Positive Reflections

What are the characteristics of a good teacher? A flair for teaching, enthusiasm for the subject, ability to communicate with children on their own level, a sympathetic regard for the individual, the ability to empathise, and a sense of humour. Children appreciate a fair adjudicator, a just disciplinarian and solid leadership. Teachers capable of acts of kindness engender endearing memories in children and set an example for the emerging adult.

'My father, Leonard Frank Flute, was born on 27 September 1911 and he went to Stagsden School. On one occasion around 1921–1923 his teacher, Mr Knott, took all the children out in the school yard to watch an eclipse, looking through pieces of smoked glass. My dad was so excited about this, he never forgot it. They also studied the stars through the vicar's telescope at the vicarage (the Rev. Jackson). Dad earned five shillings a year for pumping up the water at the vicarage, which kept him in clothes, and he talked about how he watched the Northern Lights with the bellringers at the vicarage. It was because of Mr Knott that he became so interested in astronomy that he in turn aroused in me a life-long fascination with the subject.'

JEAN FLUTE

(See Stagsden School Log, April 8, 1921, page 148)

'I was always fond of books, and was given books from school and Sunday School, as prizes. I always enjoyed school and I think the children learned more than they do now. They were strict on spelling. My mental arithmetic was good and I enjoyed doing it. The highlight of the year used to be when we went to the Eisteddfod in Bedford, which they call the Musical Festival now. There was country dancing and singing – lovely. Used to be held at the Corn Exchange and one year it was at the Town Hall.

At Souldrop School we children were sat eight or nine to a desk. The boys, little devils, took ginger pop and shook up the bottles and stood them on the window sill so they kept popping during lessons.

For the eleven-plus examination we had to go to the Bedford Drill Hall. I did well, and had the chance to go to the Girls Modern School, now called Dame Alice, but it would have meant cycling to Sharnbrook station and getting the train in, so I went to Sharnbrook School instead.

I was eleven when I went to Sharnbrook School (now called Sharnbrook Primary School – in the High Street). We all went in a lorry with a hood, which smelled of fish more often than not. That was our school transport. At Sharnbrook I had violin lessons after school, and learned to play the music by heart. My music teacher discovered that I was short-sighted which is why I memorised the music. I've worn glasses ever since.

After I left school I nursed my mother for a time as she was ill, and then went into service.'

WINIFRED ALLAN

'My first day at school (Hitchin Road Elementary School, Luton) I was given a small exercise book. I can still remember it. It was green ink and by the first story there was a picture of a woman with a mop cap on – a country hat – and it said "Dame Durdon took her eggs to market". Next picture was a lamp knocked over on the table, setting the house afire. I was about three and a half then.

Next door to the school was an iron foundry. We used to come out and watch them casting metal. It was all open fronted, the casting shop.

I left this school to go to what was once a Higher Grade School – Waller Street School. My brother had to pay so much when he went there, and it had been a private school at one time. The standard was much much higher and I was lost when I went there but it only took me a couple of years to sort of catch up. The Headmaster was a marvellous man, and I've still got a reference which he gave me dated 2 April 1914. It says "on showing intelligence, especially of late", and that my employer would find me an honest hard-working lad.

Mine was a boys schools and on one occasion they put on 'Robin Hood' and the teachers had to dress the boys up as girls, and there was quite an outcry about it. Some looked so feminine! It was quite a sensation, Maid Marion, and so on. I was a Man at Arms and a Robin Hood's Man. I had real tights but the others had to make do with ordinary breeches, cut short.'

FRANK CHAPMAN

'Mine was a first-class village school (Renhold). The Headmistress came from Norfolk and was educated at Cambridge. She used to take us on these nature lessons. We would go for a walk if the weather was right. She was a woman with discipline but she was kind. After we had been on nature study we used to have to write an essay on what we had seen. We collected leaves and plants and used these in lessons. She was a great person.

I was rather a naughty boy, disruptive and naughty. We would get the old inkwell and get a piece of blotting paper and flick it with the ruler. There were a lot of targets but many boys were good with a flicker. I have had the stick a few times, pretty hard, but she would not hold malice, one hour later you were as good as the rest. You had paid your price. She would bring the stick down hard too, but you cannot

knock it all out: we were still the same!
When we were at school there was more interest in life itself
and in nature.'

WILLIAM CONSTANT

'I started school at three, at Goldington Road School [now
Castle Lower School], which is at the top of Bower Street in
Bedford. I thought it was a lovely school, a jolly good school
with plenty of sporting activities like hockey, netball and so
on. I was Captain at one time. Mr Osborne was Headmaster
of the Senior School then. For swimming we used to go to
Newnham Baths, cutting across Russell Park. This was after
school. It was 2d or 3d for a box where you changed. If you
didn't pay at all you had to change behind a long curtain,
with racks and hooks for clothes along the wall'.

EDITH CORNWELL

'During the first year in the Infants [Milton Ernest School],
the children were allowed to sleep through part of the
afternoon until playtime. At five I entered the big classroom
where I was taught by the headmaster's daughter who took
the first three standards. [The first class, after the Infants,
was Standard 1. It was usual to test pupils to determine their
readiness for the next Standard, up to V. Some schools
provided Standard VI and VII, which were known as Higher
Standards. The majority of children left after passing the
Standard V test]. The Headmaster was a keen gardener and
we boys were taught gardening as part of the curriculum.

One of my most treasured possessions is a medal which I
won in 1912 for 'merit and conduct'.

I left school at Easter in 1914 at the age of thirteen, and
started work with my father and elder brother.'

WALTER 'REG' PARROTT

Schooldays leave an indelible mark on the memory and the soul. It is interesting to note that few of us recall individual lessons, in later life, but most have enduring memories of the teachers themselves.

Bedford Road, Wootton, as it was when Sarah attended school. On the far right is the Cock Inn, next to St. Mary's School. Mr Juff's bread delivery cart can be seen near the school, and opposite are pupils, outside Mr Redman's workshop. Photo: courtesy Mr W Juffs.

'*My first school was St. Mary's in Bedford Road, Wootton, where there now stand a row of Georgian houses which were built with the reclaimed bricks of the demolished school. Miss Tufnell and Mrs Hitchcock were my first teachers. St. Mary's belonged to the church and was originally just a Sunday School. The other Wootton school was built by Sir Phillip Payne, the local Lord of the Manor, in 1877 and I transferred to this school when I was seven. I was taught by Mr and Mrs Mepham, the Headmaster and his wife. They had two sons, Geoff and Bill. Where Stewartby now is, there was then a community called Jerusalem, and another called Pillinge, and the children walked from there all the way to school in Wootton.*'

SARAH HILLS

[In the National Society's survey in 1846 it was noted that Wootton, among other places, had only a Sunday School. At that time education was available only to the children of gentry and others in a position to pay. It was not regarded by the labouring classes as being necessary or desirable. Most 'teaching' of that period was carried out at Sunday School or in dames' cottages since it was common for children to work, at lacemaking, etc.]

COURTESY: COUNTY RECORDS OFFICE

Negative Legacies

Harsh conditions in school, coupled with negative attitudes on the part of both teacher and pupil, and intolerance of boyish misdemeanours – in particular – served to establish attitudes of resentment and indifference. Bad experiences of school also leave an indelible mark on the memory.

'I went to the Harpur Trust [Boys Elementary] School which was near the Town Hall in Bedford. I didn't care about anything except sport, and I played football for the school team. My ambition was to become a professional footballer.

It was a rough school: there were fights in the playground on numerous occasions, and the fighting often continued on the way home, and frequently turned into brutal fighting. Most of those early sparring partners of mine are dead and gone now.

For a long time whilst I was at school I did a morning newspaper round, getting up at 6am, collecting from the station, cycling to the shop to mark up and then delivering. As for lessons, I was always far too tired to concentrate on work.'

ARTHUR HARVEY

(See extracts from the Harpur Trust Boys Elementary School Log, page 150–152.)

'At Beech Hill School in Luton the children started at five, in the mixed infants, and then at seven or eight they transferred either to the Boys School or the Girls School. I attended this school from 1916 to 1920. Discipline was strict, but I had the impression that some of the boys were contented there. The Head, Mr Hackett, was brought back from retirement to teach because of the shortage of labour due to the war.

There was a section of the school known as "tin school" because of its construction.

Next to the school was an orphanage run by a charitable organisation. Boys from the orphanage who were of school age went to Beech Hill School. The orphans wore a distinctive uniform of dark grey, fairly thick material like serge. The others wore a variety of clothes as there was no uniform then. So the orphans were conspicuous and recognised as such.

One of the teachers at Beech Hill used the cane freely and the discipline at the orphanage, though reputed to have been severe, would not have been so severe when you compare it with the circumstances at that time. One mistress walked around with cane in hand looking at work. She said "stand up Horwood and hold your hand out". It was customary to punish for misbehaviour, careless and untidy work and so on. Some caned if children were late without a good excuse. On one occasion there was a small fire at a house on the way to Beech Hill which I watched. I had the cane from the Headmistress on arrival, and on arrival in the classroom, the cane from the master. They were tough times and if you came before the courts for hooliganism, you would be birched, and given six or twelve strokes.'

CLAUDE HORWOOD

'My first school was the Priory in Bedford, and I later went to Goldington Road School in Bedford [now Castle Lower School]. The only thing I can remember from school is "doh-ray-me-far-so-la-tee-doh" – every day, up and down, up and down. My music teacher must have had some influence

*on me though, as I now have a great interest in music and I
collect classical records. School days were not happy days for
me. I was the tallest and always seemed to get caught,
scrumping apples and so on, and punished. On one occasion
which I well remember, at Goldington Road School, I was
caned for being late at school. I was taken outside the
classroom and struck about six times by this teacher, Mr
Osborne. He would say "come on boy I'm going to give you
your medicine today". I ended up in hospital for six months
and needed three operations. The master was fined £5 for the
assault. I later had a cricket accident and spent a further two
months in hospital.'*

RICHARD 'THOMAS' LOVELL

The following are abstracts from the Harpur Trust Boys
Elementary School log, which make mention of Richard (then
known as Thomas Lovell). He may have been the victim of a
harsh system, but whatever the truth, he obviously created
quite a reputation for himself:

22 October 1914
A Mrs Lovell of 3 Castle Hill brought her son here for
admission. I have refused to take the boy in. He is nine years
of age and knows very little. He has a bad leg and has, it
seems, given endless trouble at Goldington Road School, in
which district he now lives. I find he has already been in
three different schools in Bedford.
3 November 1914
Mr Armstrong has brought the boy Thomas Lovell to my
school this morning. I told Mr Armstrong that I was awaiting
the final decision of the committee before admitting the boy –
for reasons I have fully laid before the committee. Mr
Armstrong says that he took the child to Goldington Road
School this morning and that Mr Osborne refused to admit
him. I have allowed the child to remain here but have not
entered his name on the books. The boy is quite well and

strong and says he can run and play easily, without any pain whatsoever, but that he is not allowed to kneel down. It is a great injustice to my staff that a boy who has given trouble should be turned out of the school and sent to another school.

26 April 1915

I regret to say that the boy Thomas Lovell of 3 Castle Hill has begun to give us trouble here. He has been playing truant five days since Easter.

According to information in Goldington Road School log, Thomas left in November 1914, when 'Mr Osborne refused to admit him'. A further entry in the log for 23 November 1914 reveals that 'The school has been commandeered for a soldiers' hospital so we close until suitable premises are found'.

'I was at the Wesleyan School in Dunstable. We 'ad an old schoolmaster there named Griffiths, and he took over Mr Graham's place when Mr Graham 'ad 'is 'olidays, you see, and if he see any of us boys talking he used to turn round and say "you sit down and hold your tongue. I'll do all the talking".

I was going up to school one day and a man said to me "ah laddy you nee'n't 'urry, the school's burnt down". They found out it was the organ started it, – the organ 'otted up. So when we got there we was all sent 'ome. Then we was notified about a month after that we'd got to go into Edward Street. We went there and then we got pushed for room so 'alf of us was sent to Chew School [in Dunstable] where the Little Theatre is now. I finished up there just before Britain Street new school was built and taking people, and I was just leaving school then. I was fourteen: it was 1910 possibly.

I worked 'ard at school and I used to get the stick nearly all the while for talking. I remember our schoolmaster he used to be a great fisherman and he used every Friday to come with one of these Golden Syrup tins pierced at the top – would I get 'im some maggots for fishing (from my father's slaughterhouse). One Friday morning he came and I said "well sir I shall 'ave a job in the slaughterhouse 'cos it wa'nt all that warm". "Well it won't matter Eric" he says "if you only get me a few I'll be much obliged". So it was three o'clock in the afternoon when I got back to school. I never liked the bloomin' teacher, he was always down on me. So he says "you go and see Mr Graham, you go for the stick". I says "it'll be you get the stick this time". I says "I'm tellin' you this". Mr Graham came in and roared out "I'm the boss 'ere: you and me'll soon part and you know who'll do the partin' don't ya", to old Bygrave. So Bygrave said to me "do you think I'd have sent you out if I'd have known that". I will say this, he was very nice to me after that.

My father 'e sent my eldest brother to the Grammar School but he wanted to be a soldier. At that time of the day soldiers were entertained as rubbish. You know, in a good many of these amusement halls they wouldn't 'ave 'em in. They used to put over the amusement halls 'dogs and soldiers not allowed'. That's right, that's true. Of course, he went and signed on: my father nearly went crackers. He said "that's what I spent on your education: put you in a brigade like that! But you're better there I daresay 'cos I can't do nothing with you". So anyway, he said to me when I was fourteen he says "you needn't worry" he says, "I ain't wastin' no money on you: I'll make you work" So he 'ad me apprenticed at Luton at Clark's Machine Tool Company.'

ERIC THORNE

'I left school at the age of thirteen, to work on the land. At the age of nine I was still being taught by the same teacher who had taught my mother, and I learned nothing during this time. Then a teacher came from Macclesfield, Cheshire. She used the cane a lot and despite the large number of children in her charge – about eighty – you could hear a pin drop. I only learned to read and write at school. In later life I joined the Workers Education Association and learned more *there than I ever did during my school years. I worked hard to improve my vocabulary, by doing the crosswords, and so on, and regard myself as being self-educated. By the age of eighteen I was secretary of the Thurleigh Cricket Club.'*

JOHN 'JACK' THORNE

Clapham School, near Bedford.

I went to Clapham School from the age of three until I was nearly twelve, then my father got a job as a gardener in Bedford and we rented a house in Dunville Road. I then went to Queens Park School for the last year and a half. We didn't have the fun that they have now. Mind you, I think it was better for us. I used to love essays and geography but if you didn't finish your composition you had to stop in after school and finish off. It was a mixed school with three classrooms. A mother and daughter looked after the infants, and when you were five you moved up into the next classroom, and later into the big room where the headmistress was in charge. She was a bitch but my brother and I cleaned her hens out every week for 3d a time. We thought if we did that she might be easier on us, but she wasn't!

Four of my brothers were in the 1914–18 war. One came home from France on leave at one time and found that I was in detention again. He came straight down to the school, walked in, fetched me out of my seat and took me home. If you misbehaved you stood outside your seat with your hands behind your back and the kids behind would tickle your hands.

The Headmistress was Miss Williams and there was Miss Haffenden, and Miss Young: her father stuffed birds and animals. Mrs Bullen and her daughter Alice, who lived in Tavistock Street, Bedford, they taught me how to knit.'

GWENDOLINE BROWN

Many elderly people remember when there was a system of mass dentistry in the schools. The children's teeth were inspected and a form sent home advising fillings and extractions as necessary, and consenting parents signed and paid one shilling for the treatment. Each child took its own shilling, and waited in trepidation as names were called out. Off they went, one by one, lambs to the slaughter, returning to class clutching bloody rags to their mouths.

On Teaching Methods

Teaching methods were as varied in years past as circumstances permitted. Practical lessons – and testing – were certainly in vogue long before the introduction of the National Curriculum! However, as every teacher knows, an essential prerequisite for effective teaching – then as now – is good discipline.

'Mr Slater was a disciplinarian. Children were lined up in a particular order before entering school and on the order "quick march" entered and stood to attention behind their forms. On the count of "one" every boy put his left leg over the form and on "two", the right one and on "three" everyone sat

down. If this was not done satisfactorily it was repeated. Boys who joined up in 1914 from our school were three-quarters trained before they saw the army!

On one occasion I had to ask Mr Slater for the afternoon off to help father pick potatoes. "Please Sir, could I have the afternoon off to pick up potatoes for my father?" "How big is this piece of potatoes?" My brain began to work overtime: five and a half square yards one rod, pole or perch. "About four poles, Sir". "How many hundredweights to the pole do you expect to get?" I had no idea. "One hundredweight, Sir" I ventured. "How many tons to the acre?" Panic again. Forty poles to the rood, four roods to the acre, a hundred and sixty poles to the acre, five tons to the acre. Was it worth it. I would sooner not have had the half-day off! He was an expert in land measuring.'

STANLEY WHITTEMORE

[Reproduced from an article in the Bedfordshire Magazine, with the publisher's permission.]

'I started school at the age of four – Stagsden School. Some children in the village began at the age of three. I walked two miles or so to school with my brothers and sisters, taking a packed lunch, as was customary at that time. School times were 9am–4pm in the summer and 9am–3.30pm in the winter, but despite the earlier leaving time in winter, it was often dusk before we got home.

Children were dealt with strictly, and wrong-doers were punished. I don't think children resented this, nor did they fear the teachers, but they did expect to be punished if they did wrong, when they were caned.

At the start of the day we children lined up on a painted line and marched in, to await the instruction to sit down. In the infants' room children sat two to a desk but in other rooms there were long desks seating about six or seven children each, with three rows. Standard I and II filled the first row, and so on up to Standards VI and VII at the rear. In the first class in the infants' room the children learned to write in sand, using a pointed stick rather like a pencil.

Each morning there was half an hour of scripture, with hymn singing and prayers. Grace was recited before dinner. After lessons in arithmetic, reading and writing there was ten minutes' play at around eleven o'clock, followed by drawing for boys and sewing for girls. Tuesdays was mental arithmetic day! There was never any homework, except on very rare occasions for those who needed to catch up or for the dunces! Each term we were set an examination. The top person became the monitor. Backward children could remain in a class and not progress to the next grade, but that rarely happened. Class seating was arranged in order of merit, according to the test results.

There were no organised games at school in my day, but football and cricket were played in the school yard. Drilling was done but this was in the form of exercises and marching, as there was no apparatus.'

HORACE WELCH

[Horace is mentioned in the Stagsden School Log, pages 146–147.)

'At Queens Park School [Bedford] which was a very small school in my time, we had benches at the front to sit on and forms at the back. There were only three classrooms. Mr Alexander was the schoolmaster and his wife was the infants' teacher. They lived in the little house on the end of the school.

I was all right at school, quite clever with arithmetic. We used to do what they called "tots", where teacher would hold up a board with numbers on it which could be turned. He would twist these numbers round and we had to count up quickly. I was always first with the answer. I wasn't much good at anything else.'

WINIFRED BURTON

I started at Goldington Road Mixed School near the rugby ground in Bedford (now called Castle Lower School) when I was four. In the Infants we used to play with a rocking horse. In all there were about six classes in each of the buildings, Infants, Juniors and Seniors.

There were big coal fires in the classrooms, which took a lot of heating in winter. Everything was formal then, and the cane was used regularly on those who stepped out of line. The teachers were older school ma'ams in those days and had to be referred to as "Miss Brown" or whatever, always using their title. We were taught manners then and our lessons took place in school – not like now, where the children are always going out and about. We did music and singing, arithmetic, reading and poetry, as I recall. I liked sport – netball, swimming and so on. For cookery we had to go into Bromham Road to a large house which was opposite Bedford High School.'

MABEL HILLYARD

School Logs

Schools which were in receipt of a government grant were – from 1863 – obliged to maintain a 'Log' detailing day-to-day events of any significance in the life of the school. Responsibility for compiling the School Log was a task encumbent on the Headteachers, and how enlightening these School Logs can be! What better way to learn something of schooldays as experienced by our parents, grandparents or great-grandparents.

The following are abstracts from the Headteacher's Log, Stagsden School:

February 26, 1906

... I was obliged to have the Infants in the main room today, as the stove is out of repair in Infant Room and there is no fire: consequently the arrangements of school are disorganised.

March 17, 1906

The weather has been very severe, and several smaller children were prevented by snow from getting to school. Work making good progress.

May 19, 1906

The average attendance has been seriously affected by a terrible gas explosion from a descending balloon, which injured seriously 6 scholars and 3 scholars have been excluded on account of mumps. The whole of the lads were removed to the hospital.   Av. 77.8.

(NB: see Contemporary Newspaper Account, page 145.)

June 2, 1906

A great number of children have been absent this week through mumps and chicken pock.

July 7, 1906

School closed for mumps.

Jul 14, 1906

School closed for mumps.

September 30, 1906

Today I resign the Mastership of Stagsden School. Signed Brighton W Gardiner.

April 15, 1908

Mr Knighton has effected an all round improvement in this school since he took charge of it . . . It appears to me to be a matter of great regret that the School Gardening has been allowed by the Managers to drop out of the Curriculum.

February 25, 1910

The Vicar The Rev. W H Jackson, presented three children with a book each for making perfect attendances during the year 1909. William Cook, Dorothy Clarke, Sidney Summerlin.

March 1, 1912

The Vicar, Rev. W H Jackson visited and checked registers. He also kindly presented prizes and certificates for attendance in year 1911. Sidney Summerlin 2nd Perfect Year's Attendance. Bar. Endorsement and Book.

THE BEDFORDSHIRE TIMES AND INDEPENDENT, FRIDAY, MAY 18, 1906

Balloon Descent at Stagsden

SERIOUS ACCIDENT

SEVERAL PEOPLE INJURED

Stagsden received a most unusual visitor from the skies on Saturday evening, when the balloon which had been seen to pass over Bedford a little earlier descended. About 6.40pm, the balloon was spied high in the heavens coming at a good rate from towards Bedford, and very soon almost every man, woman, and child in the place were directing their optics skyward. The balloon was then apparently between Hangers' Wood and Astey Wood, and having crossed the village street close to the church, it was seen to be descending fast, with grappling rope plainly descernible. Off trooped the whole village, none stopping to lock doors or place the house under police protection. Nor did they keep to the highway or footpaths, but hurried straight across country, and pellmell over hedge and ditch. In the third field one man seized the dangling rope, but the psychological moment was not yet, and he had to cling tight as he was carried over into the next field, which is on Mr Landon's farm at North End, where the descent was completed.

The balloon, we are informed, bore the world-famed name of 'Spencer,' and in large letters the words 'Vivienne III.' According to a London contemporary, Mr E Rider Cook made an ascent in this balloon on Saturday afternoon at 2.30, from the Crystal Palace. He was alone in the car, making the 'solo' trip necessary to qualify as a pilot of the 'Aeronaut Club,' and adds the report, 'an excellent descent was made at Bedford.' Mr Cook was soon out of the car, and the work of releasing the gas was immediately in hand. The crowd was continually augmented by fresh arrivals from the villages around, and included the Kempston Cricket team, which had just finished its game with the Stagsden players. The crowd must eventually have well exceeded a hundred. Everything was proceeding merrily as marriage bells, young and old, enjoying the novelty, especially the rythmic rising and falling of the 'gas-bag' as they rolled about the balloon to help drive out the gas, until about 7.30, when a hissing noise, somewhat resembling that made by a steam exhaust pipe, was heard, and several people seemed to fall. It was at first thought that Mr Cook had liberated the gas from another aperture, and there was a peal of laughter, in which the injured ones joined with the rest, at what was thought to be a practical joke to get them clear, but very quickly the serious reality became apparent and when the first feeling of numbness had passed off, the sufferings of those who had caught the full force of the explosion was intense, and their faces and hands were a fearful sight, being described by some witnesses as more like old parchment, with big blisters, than anything else.

Exactly how the explosion was caused is not known, but it is believed that one of the bystanders struck a match to light his pipe and, without thinking threw it on to the ground within the area where the gas was diluted or not sufficiently diluted with the air. Mr Cook had several times warned them against this sort of thing, but the balloon spread about a good way, and it was possible that some would not hear him. In fact, quite a number of those present say they did not hear any mention of the matter. Immediately upon hearing the noises, Mr Cook shouted out for someone to jump on the valve, and a young man, whom report saith was one of the Kempston cricketers, and is employed at the Kempston gas-house, heroically responded, and at imminent risk to himself threw his full weight upon it thus shutting it down and stopping the supply. How near they were to a most appalling catastrophe those present probably never realised, for had the flame got to the gas in the balloon, to use Mr Cook's works, they 'must all have been blown to smithereens'. Fortunately, Mr Cook's presence of mind and the cricketer's quick response averted a greater calamity.

Attention was at once turned to the injured ones, who had made off to the village, about a quarter of a mile distant. Some went to the house of Mr Bonnett where the ambulance requisites are always kept ready for an emergency. Dr Green of Turvey, was sent for, and in the meantime the Ambulance Class, including Mrs Bonnett, Mrs Babbington, Mrs Linger and Mrs Fanny Riddy did their best to assuage the pain with carron oil and lint. Two of the boys, however, made for Mr Landon's house, and here P.c. Steers and Miss Wells gave them first aid. One little fellow ran to a brook in an adjacent field, and washed his face, with the result that flesh came off when he wiped it with his handkerchief. He was a most pitiable sight, and must have suffered indescribable agony. Having done what he could, Dr Greene ordered the sufferers to the County Hospital. Mr John Wright having considerately been over to make arrangements, and returned with conveyances from Bedford. The Vicar, the Rev. S A Spooner, Mr Wright, Mr H Newman, Mr, Mrs and Miss Dimmock, Mr W Pettit, and Mr F Ellis were most assiduous in their attentions to the injured. Those most seriously affected were: Joseph Fuller, horse-keeper, aged 36, Thomas Riddy, stonemason, 25; W Wright (Astwood) 15; Herbert Beard 11; Leonard Beard 8; Samuel Wright 13; William Clark 11; and Fredk. Henson, aged 12. Seven of them were taken to the Hospital. Mr Riddy, who was not so badly burned as the rest, was treated at home. Many others were scorched or singed more or less badly.

The Vicar wishes us to state that he has opened a subscription list. Fuller is a married man with a numerous family of little ones, and the others belong to the labouring class. Contributions will be gratefully acknowledged by him.

Mr Cook was uninjured and returned to London by the M R from Bedford about 10pm on Saturday night. He visited the sufferers before leaving, and expressed sympathy with them. The calamity is regarded as purely accidental, and no blame is cast upon Mr Cook. On Sunday, expressions of sympathy were made from the pulpits of the church and chapel.

The Rev. W H Jackson has received from Mr E R Cook a letter, addressed from Cecilhurst, Uplands Park, Enfield asking the Vicar to be so kind as to let him know how the patients are progressing as, although it was not his fault, he felt responsible in a measure for the accident. He was always careful to see that no one smoked near a balloon, but one could not be everywhere at the same time.

On inquiry at the Hospital on Thursday morning, we were informed that all the patients are making excellent progress, and hopes are now entertained of the lad Henson's, recovery.

145

March 27, 1912

Only 32 present owing to Oakley Hunt 'Point to Point Races' being held in the village . . . Most of the parents sent word to me that they sanctioned their children's absence from school.

April 17, 1912

The Wreck of the Titanic was (also) made the subject of special lessons.

February 19, 1913

Gave lessons on Antarctic Expedition. Heroism of brave explorers.

March 2, 1914

Mrs Whitmee, wife of the Correspondent, visited school this afternoon, and presented the prizes awarded to Scholars for Progress, etc. during 1913, as follows. Walsh, Alice M. (Captain), Wright F, Linger B, Darlow Ivy, Darlow Walter, Lilley Violet, Knott M B, Bonnett P C and Welch H. Have posted 'Roll of Honour' or list of Prize-winners.

July 7, 1914

By kind permission of Mr J W Warboys, a relative of mine, I was able to exhibit several nuggets of Gold, from places as widely apart as Kalgoorlie, Coolgardie, etc. and Eldorado Creek, Klondyke.

October 30, 1914

During the progress of the War I have occasionally given brief descriptions of the main movements and events. Pictures have also been utilised and maps for reference.

November 2, 1914

Pamphlets on 'The War' received from Ed. Office, read and discussed and explained where necessary. The collection of Patriotic Verse sent will also be made use of.

January 14, 1915

I received instructions from the military authorities to present myself Medically Fit for Military Service this morning. I have informed the Managers through the Correspondent of this fact.

January 18, 1915
. . . One boy, S Summerlin, away at Agric. work being over 12 years of age.
June 14, 1915
Mr J Barnett, MR San. I. gave a lecture to the Mixed Dept. on 'Alcohol and the Human Body' this afternoon.
July 15, 1915
Owing to Beds. County Agricultural Show being held at Bromham, a number of children are absent today.
September 6, 1915
Re-opened school after Harvest Holidays. Only 42 present out of 79 on Books. Have informed Correspondent.
September 7, 1915
Received instructions from Correspondent, Mr A J Whitmee, that if no considerable improvement in numbers present this morning, to close school until Monday September 13, 1915. As there were only 43 present this was done.
September 13, 1915
Re-opened . . . 59 present.
February 4, 1916
Several cases of Diptheria have occurred. Med. Officer of Health visited school and authorised closing for a fortnight.
May 19, 1916
School closed by Dr Welch, School Medical Officer owing to outbreak of Scarlet Fever in the School House.
June 19, 1916
. . . At present there are 3 children . . . and Amy Askew (Monitress) at the Isolation Hospital with Scarlet Fever.
August 9, 1916
A further case of Scarlet Fever has occurred (Hilda Welch) and another suspected (Horace Welch) . . .
August 10, 1916
. . . Dr Moore, Acting Medical Officer of Health visited school and advised immediate closure of school.
September 13, 1916
Received call to Military Service for September 25 1916

and must therefore temporarily relinquish my position as Head Teacher of Stagsden School.

June 2, 1920

Four children absent attending County Minor Scholarship Examination, Bedford.

June 3, 1920

Four children absent attending Free Place (Secondary) Schools Examination, Bedford.

June 24, 1920

. . . Two of the children who entered the Free Place (Secondary) Schools Examination . . . have been instructed to appear for Oral Examinations in Bedford today.

April 8, 1921

Watched Annular Eclipse and at the Vicar's invitation the children marched down to the Vicarage to view eclipse through a large telescope.

July 15, 1921

Received intimation from the Clerk of the Harpur Trust that Stanley L W Knott has been awarded *a Free Place* at *Bedford School.*

Stagsden School pupils and staff, circa 1919.
Photo: courtesy Herbert Welch (sitting on floor, on left).

Marriage of The Duke and Duchess of York, 26 April 1923.
(Elizabeth Bowes-Lyon and 'Bertie' – Albert Frederick Arthur
George, crowned George VI on 12 May 1937).
Photo: courtesy The Illustrated London News Picture Library.

July 29, 1921

Prizes for Year 1920–1921 presented this morning upon the occasion of the school closing at noon for the Harvest Holidays 5 weeks.

Prize Winners: Knott S L W, Darlow R, Welch Annie, Harris Ronald, Myers Fred, Burley Frank, Newman George, Welch Herbert, Linger Gladys.

September 30, 1921

Attendance much poorer this week owing in part to cases of exclusion for Whooping Cough and Fever.

February 27, 1922

Tomorrow a day's Holiday 'Princess Mary's Wedding Day' has been given.

April 24, 1923

Received notification of Holiday for Thursday April 26 according to the expressed wish of the King, in honour of the marriage of The Duke of York.

December 21, 1923

School closed for Xmas Holidays at noon. Distributed a wide assortment of Novelties among the children. To each child Mr Arnold kindly presented a bag of dates (sent to him by his son from Persia) and Mrs Knott gave each an orange.

January 15, 1924

As the marriage of our late U. [Uncertificated] Assistant (Miss A M Babbington) in the Infants Department takes place at a time coinciding with our play time I allowed the children to go down to the church then to see the bride leave the church after the ceremony.

Here are some extracts not from a village school, but from a school situated in town, – the Harpur Trust Boys Elementary School in Bedford:

24 February 1915

Punished Bertie Izzard and Lewis Gower for running out of school at playtime. 4 strokes on latter end in the presence of class master.

25 February 1915

Mrs Cox visited school to complain of her grandson's punishment. She admitted that her two charges, . . . , run wild in the street. They came to school filthy and I had one of them before her. She declared that it was the natural colour of his skin.

14/15 March 1915

Punished Herbert Gough. 6 strokes on latter end in presence of Mr Ball, for truanting several times (class 6).

Punished Leslie George (ditto above) (class IV) – truant since Christmas on and off.

Punished Herbert Crossley – 4 strokes – truanting. His mother has been to see me and reports great difficulty at home with Herbert, as she has to work early. (Class 5).

16 March 1915

Punished Hull, Jenkins and Fowkes, Class 1, for playing truant.

12/15 April 1915

There are a large number of boys away who should be at school and very many are playing truant. Boys Gough, Fowkes, L George and Lovell all with the knowledge of their respective mothers . . .

19 April 1915

The truant officer has again brought Leslie George. . . . 2 Goughs, Swift and Conquest are here again, all having been brought by their mother or Mr Armstrong.

21 June 1915

Punished R Fowkes for truancy, 4 strokes. This boy is exceedingly defiant to his teacher and very impudent. I should be glad if an example could be made of him. The whole family has given us great trouble.

[Author's note: Despite the extent of truancy and its consequences, teaching obviously has its rewards. Success in scholarship examinations, the opportunities this presented for working class children, and the pride and sense of achievement it afforded to teaching staff, parents and pupils alike, must have resulted in renewed optimism for the education system.]

16 July 1915

Exhibitions (10 given) in Bedford. I have received from the Clerk to the Harpur Trust a communication stating that 5 boys have obtained £10 exhibitions tenable at the Modern School.

The less academic were also given opportunities to succeed, in sporting and competitive events, the like of which are now discouraged.

29 July 1915

The Swimming Prizes – given by old boys of the school . . . were competed for last Tuesday. . . . 55 boys entered for the races. The prizes were:
    fishing rods and tackle
    watches and chains
    clocks and
    fountain pens
The boys enjoyed the races greatly and keen competition was shown.

The summer holiday obviously provided teaching staff with time for reflection and planning, and renewed optimism. 'Appraisal' may appear to present-day educationalists to be a fashionable and innovative phenomenon, but there is ample evidence to suggest that it has been practiced since the early days of compulsory education. One example from the Harpur Trust Boys Elementary School Log follows:

13 October 1915

I have now obtained a complete syllabus of work to be done by each class, from each master, before the work is actually done.

It is my intention to sign each syllabus of work. This will co-ordinate the work and I hope, improve the methods of teaching.

COURTESY: COUNTY RECORDS OFFICE

Absenteeism

Illness was a major cause of absence from school, although the indications are that children – boys and girls – were frequently kept away from school in order to help in the home or on the land. Maternal illness frequently meant that the eldest girl would be required to help with the household chores and possibly in caring for infant siblings. However, there is also evidence to show that parents often made every effort to enable children to attend school regularly. (See Stagsden School Log Book, March 1, 1912, page 144.)

'My eldest sister started school in Knotting, but it was eventually closed and we all had to go to school in Souldrop. We went in a horse-drawn covered waggon belonging to Mr Lamb, who lived in Souldrop. This was the 'school bus'. You could run across the fields and catch it at Souldrop Turn if you were late.

I started school at the age of three and mother used to send me off with my white starched 'pinney' on, with a handkerchief pinned to it.

I reckon we must have stank to high heaven at times, with the goose grease, thermagine and camphorated oil which mother used to rub on our chests for colds and chest ailments. This was before the days of Vick, which was equally as potent. I had rheumatic fever soon after starting school and yellow jaundice but mother nursed me through these illnesses. Scarlet fever or diptheria meant going to Clapham Isolation Hospital. My sister went there with it. If one member of the family was ill, all the other children in the family had to stay away too. If infectious illnesses were present the house had to be fumigated. I think they used to do it with a camphor candle, and the house was sealed up until the candle burned out.'

WINIFRED ALLAN

'My father was a rag and bone man, and I often went with him on his house rounds. I had to help with the horses, and often took them to the blacksmith in Milton Ernest to be re-shod. This meant taking time off school. I had each Friday off school too – which I was allowed – because my mother was ill and I had to help her in the house.

When I was eleven I started to help my father in the rag house, sorting and bagging up, but this was after school. By the time I was twelve I was driving the horse and trolley into Bedford, to make deliveries.'

IVY FLUTE

The School Leaver

At the turn of the century the official school leaving age was set at 13 years. However, with the huge numbers of men conscripted for military service during the First World War, the need for labour on the land, in industry and munitions, became a matter of governmental concern. Women were encouraged to work, and boys could obtain a Labour Certificate enabling them to leave school at the age of 12 years, provided work were available to them on the land, and providing they could pass a leaver's examination, demonstrating that they had reached a certain standard of education.

'Schooldays are the best days of your life' the adage goes. Not all would agree no doubt, but the experience leaves a marked impression on everyone, and enduring memories.

'When I was eleven years and six months old I sat for my School Exam at Sharnbrook, to gain my Work Certificate. I well remember my Headmistress calling me to her desk on the Friday at the Close of school and giving me a real talking to about the exam that I was to take on the following Saturday. She impressed on me that I was quite able to pass the exam if I would only concentrate. She pointed out to me that colossal

task my parents had, to feed and clothe such a large family, and if I passed the exam and gained my Work Certificate I would be able to start work and earn some money to help my parents. I was very determined to do the best I could, after listening to her lecture. She then put her hand on my shoulder and said "now don't let me down Fred. I am sure you can do it, and I shall have a share in your success too".

I sat for the exam and found it fairly easy on all the subjects. One was that we had to write a letter to the Examiner about our family life. I had quite a lot to say about that subject and had to ask the inspector for some more paper. I mentioned in it I had three sisters and three brothers and did want to pass this exam so that I could start work and earn some money. He picked up my paper and read the letter I had written. His comment on the size of the family was "poor man, I pity him". "That's a really good letter my boy", he said, "I wish I could write one like it". He suggested I should go to work on a newspaper. Yes, I passed the exam and gained my Work Certificate but I was supposed to keep on at school until I was twelve years old but I did not go to school anymore and we heard no more about it. Mrs Hebbs was pleased and said "I knew you could do it". Now I was a British workman!'

FREDERICK WILDMAN

'School leaving age was thirteen but by the time I was due to leave it had been raised to fourteen. Many children took the "Labour Examination" and if successful could leave early and go to work on the farm, or in the case of the girls, go into service. I took mine at the age of twelve. This was held at the old Bedford Modern School in Midland Road [now a part of the Harpur Centre]. It consisted of sums, reading, composition (I wrote about Stagsden Church), spellings, etc. I left at the age of thirteen, having passed this examination.

Since the age of eight I had worked Saturday and holidays on the farm and it was a foregone conclusion that I would work on the farm after leaving school – there were always jobs waiting. I started work with my father and continued to be a farm worker until the age of 56, when ill-health meant I could no longer continue.'

HORACE WELCH

'I cannot remember a time when I was not made to work on my father's farm. From the age of seven I had always helped at harvest time, carting corn and leading the horses. It was a mixed farm, and I looked after the animals and did almost everything that father did. It was always my ambition and intention to return to the farm after leaving school, and this is what I did, at the age of sixteen.'

JOHN CAMPION
BEDFORD MODERN PUPIL

Alternative Education

There were – for a minority of children – alternatives to attending the local state school. Some of the more affluent members of the community employed a Governess; others opted for private education. Children fortunate enough to win scholarships could attend the Harpur Trust endowed schools in Bedford.

'My introduction to education was with a governess, and then after two or three years at Souldrop School I went to Bedford Modern School. It then became necessary to cycle to the station in Sharnbrook each day and catch the train into Bedford. Country boys were termed by their classmates the "train boys" and were in a sense socially segregated from the mainstream, comprising boarders and town boys. The "train boys" perceived themselves as being different, and were in a class of their own.

The education at Bedford Modern School was very academic with emphasis being placed on sporting prowess, particularly at cricket and rugger. For the "train boys" the school day was a lengthy one, as sporting activities often took place while it was light, with a return to the classroom for lessons. With the time taken travelling, we often arrived home as late as 7pm, which seemed an exceptionally long day to a young lad.'

JOHN CAMPION

'My mother was a pupil at Miss Bates School for business people's children, which was near the old Bedford Modern School. The charge was one shilling a week, and they were issued with a slate and slate pencil. She used to go to school in the pony and trap and she told me that there were only cart tracks then down Harpur Street and in that area. At the end of the day Dobbin, her horse, would be waiting for her outside the school – he was always pleased to see her. Her father was strict and used to want to see the slate which she had used in lessons. She dare not smudge it or she would get into trouble!'

EDITH 'IRENE' CORNWELL

'Mr Lucas was the scholarship teacher and he took the scholarship class. You had to take an examination and then an interview for the Girls Modern School, the Boys Modern School, the Girls High School and Bedford School. There were quite a few scholarships won from our school. Parents got a grant for clothes and books but it was not enough. Braggins (now Beales) in Bedford, supplied the clothes and parents were given samples of the materials and they had to buy identical clothes from this store, which could be very expensive. My brother and my nephew both won scholarships. My nephew said the grant was not enough and he found it difficult mixing with the boys who were not working class. He's a teacher now.'

MABEL HILLYARD

'I thoroughly enjoyed my time at Howard College in Bedford, which was a private establishment. Even if you were not academic, which I was not, it gave you a sense of self-importance, confidence. It taught you etiquette. There were many things you learned which you would otherwise have not, unless you were from a good family. It has enabled

me to stand up for myself. The girls there were lovely, a nice type of girl from professional families, business families. There were girls from America, Jamaica and other places. We only went home at the end of term, but we loved boarding school life.

There was so much variety at school. There was prep. time, time for music, prayers and hymns each day, reading from the Bible. We did French and German at Howard College, which were not part of the state school curriculum. Every Friday night there was a dance and the Head Girl would play the piano. Boys were not allowed to come, of course. I took up ballet dancing. You had to pay extra for these things, naturally. There were many things to choose from including horse riding. There were sports on the court in the school grounds but we went to Russell Park for hockey as there was not a lot of space for sports at the school. We went to the Commercial Baths for swimming.

We could sit the Junior or Senior Cambridge Entrance Examination and some of the girls did this. There were termly examinations and reports, but no final examinations. There were no vocational studies, but it was a good all-round education. I left at the age of sixteen.'

EDITH INKSON

'My parents engaged a Governess who was charged with the responsibility of educating my sisters and me. There was some considerable animosity between us, and mutual dislike. A punishment favoured by our Governess, for being naughty, was to be shut in a cupboard under the stairs. To this day all three of us suffer from claustrophobia as a result.

We had a nursery- and school-room at Wootton House [in the village of Wootton] and we children were brought up very strictly. Mother was not aware of – or did not wish to be involved in – the conflict between her children and the Governess. Each day followed a set pattern, with work in the morning, a brisk walk, followed by lunch, and then a further walk. Three or four hours each day were spent out of the

Wootton House.
Photo: courtesy Allot & Barnard and Knight, Frank & Rutley.

house walking, until I told my father that we were not learning anything. He agreed to my request that we be allowed to go away to school. My two younger sisters went as weekly boarders to schools in Bedford and I went to boarding school at Beaconsfield, but ran away and returned home after the first week! This happened twice, after which time I was sent to Crescent House Ladies College in Linden Road, Bedford. I quite enjoyed this experience, and left at sixteen and went on to attend Gloucester School of Economics for one year, to do a practical course in home economics. I graduated with a diploma.'

EYVOR PELHAM REID

'My twin sister and I shared a governess until I went to Preparatory School at Little Appley on the Isle of Wight at the age of eight. Victorian attitudes to child-rearing were still prevalent at the time, (1928), and it was considered a good thing for children to be raised in the exhilarating fresh sea

air. *Although I was homesick to begin with I came to enjoy boarding school life. Being on the Solent there were frequently big liners to be seen passing by, such as the Queen Mary and Queen Elizabeth, the Sneider Trophy Races and so on, so it was all very different and exciting. After leaving Preparatory School I was sent to Uppingham in Rutland.'*

OLIVER WELLS

Board of Education.
Form 146 (a).

Local Education Authority for____Bedfordshire._____

LABOUR CERTIFICATE No. 1.

AGE AND EMPLOYMENT. PROFICIENCY.

I certify that _Edith Annie Wagstaff_ ,   I certify that _Edith Annie Wagstaff_

residing at _Thurleigh_ ,   residing at _Thurleigh_ ,

was on the _8th_ day of _December_ 190_, not   has received a certificate from _C.G. Colson Esq_

less than twelve years of age, having been born on the _1st_ day   one of His Majesty's Inspectors of Schools, that he (or she) has (3) reached the

of _August_ 18_92_, as appears by the registrar's   _fourth_ Standard.

certificate [or the statutory declaration] now produced to me, (1) and has been shown to

the satisfaction of the local authority for this district to be beneficially employed.

(Signed) _Frank Spooner_

Wm. W. Marks   Principal Teacher of the School.

(Signed)   Director of Education.

(1) Clerk to the Education Committee of the above Authority.   or (2) Clerk to the Education Committee of the above Authority.

(1) Strike out what follows if the child is qualified for full time employment.   (3) To reach a standard a child must be individually examined in reading, writing, and arithmetic
(2) Or other officer.   in that or a higher standard, and must pass in each of those subjects.

Labour Certificate issued to Edith Wagstaff, aged 12 years, in December 1904.
Courtesy: Mr E Wildman, Thurleigh.

CONTRIBUTORS

WINIFRED LOUISA ALLAN (NÉE HODBY)

Winnie was born at Knotting Green on 8 January 1919. Her father and his father were also born there, in a tied cottage near the church. Her father spent all his working life on Green Farm, owned by Mr Pike. There were no privately owned properties in the village at that time. Of the six children born to Winnie's parents, one died at the age of twelve with appendicitis.

Winnie's family have always been active church members. Her grandfather was an organist and her father too, both self-taught. One vicar (Rev. Wiggins) looked after two parishes then, Knotting and Souldrop. Most village people were church-goers and at harvest festival and the Knotting Feast the church would be packed to capacity.

Winnie met her husband in Bedford in 1938. He was in the Airforce training at Cardington, but he came from Scotland. He was posted to Mildenhall but they kept in touch and were married on New Year's Eve, 1941. As a time-serving airman, he saw action in the Second World War, and was invalided out in 1944.

GWENDOLINE ELSIE BROWN (NÉE JEFFRIES)

Gwen was born in Clapham on 16 June 1908. Her father was a gardener and gravedigger and for ten years of his life he worked solely as a gravedigger at Bedford Cemetery. Gwen's parents had twelve children, of whom nine survived. Four of her brothers were in the first world war.

Gwen met her husband whilst in service at Sharnbrook, and married at the age of twenty. They had seven children. He was a farm worker having worked for some years at Samuel Whitbread's farm near Shefford, and also at Hill Farm, Chellington, but ill health forced him to leave the farm and he then got a job with the Ministry at Twinwoods (from where Glen Miller took off on his last fated flight).

Gwen's husband died in 1968.

WINIFRED BURTON (NÉE POULTER)

Winnie was born on 1 October 1909 in Cricket Lane, Bedford, in a thatched cottage which has since disappeared. Her parents moved to School Yard when she was about three, at the back of Barkers Lane and near to Goldington School. Winnie's father was a sheet metal worker at Allens, as was his father. There were three children in the family.

Winnie was married at twenty-four, to a painter, decorator and signwriter, and continued to work only as a holiday relief, until her son was born.

JOHN ALFRED CAMPION

John was born on 15 October 1907 at Manor Farm, Knotting. His father was a local man and a farmer: his mother lived in Peterborough before her marriage, but had relatives in Sharnbrook and so was no stranger to this area. They had six children, two boys and four girls.

Farming has always been John's main interest. There was a time when he could have started his own farm, but he chose to spend much of his time caring for his invalid sister, a one-time pupil at Bedford High School. He established an enterprise as an agricultural haulier. The business did well and there was always work to be had. He retired 14 years ago. He believes he made as much money with his lorries as many of the farmers did farming their land.

FRANK PERCY CHAPMAN

Frank was born on 3 March 1900 at 31 Ashton Street, Luton, where he lived until he was married at twenty-three. His mother didn't want him to have a motor for the wedding, so he had to get a carriage and pair of greys. Powdrill did the wedding (they were building contractors and had a farm) and as Frank lived only two minutes from the church, they were driven right round the town before actually going into church.

Rudds, where his mother worked, did the wedding cake, for which they charged two pounds: Frank thought it was worth five at least! He regarded this as a favour, since they were friends and neighbours.

On the occasion of his Diamond Wedding Anniversary, Frank and his wife received a telegram from the Queen, of which he is very proud.

WILLIAM CONSTANT

Bill's father was born in Bedfordshire, but Bill was born on 29 July 1916 at Hessett, near Bury St. Edmunds, Suffolk, his mother being a Suffolk woman. There were three children in the family, two boys and one girl, but Bill's brother, the last-born of the children, died of meningitis when he was four or five. Bill was nearly five when his parents came to live in Renhold,

EDITH IRENE ELIZABETH CORNWELL (NÉE CROWSLEY)

Edith was born in Dudley Street, Bedford, on 16 February, 1910. Her parents later moved to Bower Street, near the embankment. She has always been known as 'Irene'.

Irene's husband was related to Jack Cornwell VC, who was in the Royal Navy. She and her husband had six children, and she now has sixteen grandchildren and eleven great grandchildren. She has been widowed for twenty-eight years, enjoyed her married life but is now quietly contented and has never wanted to re-marry: thinks she is old-fashioned!

CHRISTOPHER JOHN CREAMER

Chris was born on 14 December 1903 at Church End, Milton Bryan. His father was a woodman/forester on the Woburn estate. Their home was a charity cottage, belonging to the Milton Bryan Charity. Chris's grandfather, Levi Creamer, worked on Manor Farm, which was part of the Battlesden estate. His mother played the organ at the local church from the time she was nine years old, and her mother – Grandmother Clark – who had always lived in Milton Bryan, died at the age of 97.

Chris officially retired at 65, but received no pension, and has worked since then for a local farmer, hedging and ditching, and helping with the cows.

ELSIE ROSE ENGLAND

Elsie was born on 1 July 1905 at 44 High Street South, Dunstable. The property – her parents' home and bakery – was on the corner of High Street South and Britain Street, and the house is now occupied by a firm of accountants.

In her younger days, Elsie worked for a Dunstable firm of herbalists known as Flemons and later called Flemons and Marchant. They employed men to collect dandelion roots, comfry leaves, foxgloves and so on, which were sold to wholesalers for drug houses. They also made their own herbal medicine.

Dunstable was a relatively small place in Elsie's youth, and everybody knew everybody else.

IVY FLUTE (NÉE LAWSON)

Ivy was born on 16 February 1916 at Radwell, a hamlet near Felmersham. Her father was the local rag-and-bone merchant, known as 'Raggy Lawson'.

Ivy's father collapsed and died after a trip to London, in 1950, aged 72. Ivy inherited enough money to send her son to Bedford Modern School and he went on to university and is now a teacher. She remembers her father with admiration and affection.

ARTHUR RICHARD HARVEY

Arthur was born on 14 October 1911 in Greyfriars Walk, Bedford. His father was a boxer at one time, and was for many years a market trader, trading in seafoods.

Arthur has had an assortment of jobs over the years, but only took these to fit in with his boxing interests and to support himself. He spent four years at Robertsons and six years at Allens in Coventry during the war, making aircraft parts and munitions. He was in the Home Guard, the RAF and later the Royal Navy. He joined the Merchant Navy for a time in 1949 and visited Australia twice during this time.

HILDA HAYDEN

Hilda was born in St. Cuthbert, Bedford, on Boxing Day of 1894, and was the last of eleven children. Her father had his own decorating business, and she thinks the family were comfortably-off. The large house in Newnham Street where she grew up, had four bedrooms with two large reception rooms downstairs and a lobby.

During Hilda's courting days she and her sisters were only allowed to take boyfriends home when they had decided if they 'wanted them'. One of her friends became pregnant, and she and her sisters Alice and Connie were told quite bluntly that if anything like that happened to them, father would not have them in the house. She was twenty-nine when she married, but she was a good girl!

SARAH ANN HILLS (NÉE LOWE)

Sarah was born on 3 October 1900 in Cause End Road, Wootton, next door to the shop and the Star Public House. This property has since been demolished. Her grandmother's home was one of the four Yeoman's Cottages at Chennell's Farm, then owned by Mr Frossell, and it was from there that her mother moved to Cause End Road to live following her marriage. When Sarah was a year old her parents moved to Keeley, Wootton. Both parents were from Wootton, and father was a thatcher by trade. Sarah was only three years old when he died of pneumonia, leaving her mother to raise four children, Sarah being the youngest.

MABEL DORIS HILLYARD (NÉE STANTON)

Mabel was born on 12 December 1913 in Priory Street, Bedford. She had one brother. Her father, Walter Stanton, was a blacksmith. He traded in Commercial Road, where the Council works were. He was actually employed by the Corporation and did all the ironwork for Bedford, all the fancy gates. He was in the army during the First World War and during this time her mother often went out scrubbing floors. He suffered from dysentry whilst in the forces, and his weight reduced to six stone at one time, but he survived the war and returned to his smithy, where he worked for forty-eight years in all.

CLAUDE HORWOOD

Claude was born at 41 Biscot Road, Luton, on 7 August 1911. His grandfather was a chemist in Dunstable, and later worked at the Wootton and Webb pharmacy. He then had his own shop in Brunswick Street, Luton. Claude's father was apprenticed to Harts Hat manufacturers and he eventually left Harts and started in business on his own as a travelling peddler of hats. As a hat salesman, he was unsuccessful. He travelled around by train, and Claude's mother told him that there was so little profit that once he had bought his three-monthly season ticket, there was very little left. Claude's mother was a machinist in the hat trade.

HELENA MIRIAM HUDSON (NÉE DIX)

Miriam, as she was always called, was born in Clophill on 5 May 1915. Her father died in Leighton Buzzard in 1915, three months before she was born. She had three brothers. Her mother then returned to live with her parents who ran the village stores at Clophill. Miriam's mother died in 1918 in the 'flu epidemic. Her grandmother told her that her mother earned about nine shillings a week as a dress-maker, doing piece work, before she died, and was trying to raise four children on that. After her mother's death, her grandparents officially fostered Miriam and her brothers.

Miriam's grandfather, (her mother's father), Henry Daniels lost a hand in a sawmill accident, and was awarded compensation. This is how he started the first business. Her grandmother, Pricilla Daniels, lived to be 86 and died when Miriam was thirteen (she was raised in Maulden, attended a Dame School and did hat work at home, for Luton factories): Henry Daniels died in 1928. Miriam has a photograph of Clophill, in which can just be seen the window of the room where she was born. This was the Clophill Post Office. Another photograph shows Emily and Lilian, her aunts, and a nextdoor neighbour.

EDITH INKSON (NÉE COLLINS)

Edith was born in Northamptonshire on 28 October 1910, and came to live with her spinster aunt at Bury End, which was about a mile and a half from Stagsden, when she was twelve, following the death of her parents. Her father was killed when he was thrown from a pony and trap in Rushden, where he was in business manufacturing shoes, and her mother died of pernicious anaemia.

There were seven children in the family, but the eldest boy died of meningitis, leaving three boys and three girls, two of whom were twins (Edith and Grace).

MARY JEFFS (NÉE COOLING)

Mary was born on 26 December 1893 in West Bromwich, Staffordshire, and came to Bedford in the 1920s to stay with an aunt who was living in Kempston. She only came for a holiday, but loved the place so much that she decided to stay. West Bromwich was the Black Country, all coal mines, and Bedford seemed a complete change, to her.

Mary's mother died at the age of twenty-five, when Mary was a young child, and she was raised by her father's mother in Warwickshire. She thinks her father worked in the iron foundries but is not sure. He was in the First World War and returned, but didn't live long afterwards. She was his only child.

Mary's grandfather was a farm worker. Her grandparents' home was in Butlers Marston, just a little hamlet about nine miles from Stratford-on-Avon. This was hunting country, and the local hunt was the Warwickshire hounds. Lord Willoughby de Broke had a large country estate there: he did a lot of private work for the Queen Mother.

RICHARD THOMAS LOVELL

Richard, who was always known as Tom, was born at The Folleys in Clapham in August 1904, and was one of twelve children. Tom's family were keen sports people, but because of leg injuries sustained in his younger days, Tom was never able to participate. One brother was a well-known professional boxer.

STANLEY GEORGE LOVELL

Stan was born on 9 March 1909 in Hall End, Wootton. He was one of three children, and his father was a general labourer – a bricklayer's labourer – who worked at the brickworks and for Samuel Foster, the builders in Kempston, where Bushbys are now situated. He also worked for Mr Lunnis, the builder at 'Tags End' which is now called Cause End Road. After leaving school at fourteen, Stan worked at the local brickworks for many years.

Stan was in the St. John's Ambulance Brigade for twenty-five years, at Stewartby and then at Kempston, and only left the Brigade in 1954, when he was diagnosed as having a brain tumour. He received medical training in Sidmouth, Devon and was a male nurse with the RAF at Weeton near Blackpool and then at North Allerton, until he was demobbed. He helped to set it up, in North Allerton, and was there when the first patient arrived. It was like a general hospital for the Air Force. He chose this career course with the RAF because of his experience in the St. John's Ambulance Brigade.

ETHEL ANNIE MAYES (NÉE JARVIS)

Ethel was born in Luton on 30 August 1899. Her mother died when she was three, and, left with a family of six children, her father re-married. His second wife had been employed as a housekeeper in a big house. She looked after Annie and brought her up well: 'she was a very good person'. There were no children from this second marriage.

Ethel's husband had always worked for his uncle, who had a shop in Hastings Street (now the site of a block of offices) called Rumblows. They did watch and clock repairs. The uncle had no children and when he died he left the business to Ethel's husband. She and her two sons continued to run it for quite some time after the death of her husband. It was well-known locally.

WALTER REGINALD PARROTT

Walter, who has always been known as Reg, was born on 28 January 1901 in a stone and thatched cottage in the village of Milton Ernest.

Reg married in 1927 and set up home in Thurleigh. In 1959 he and his wife acquired a sixteen acre smallholding in Keysoe and planned to grow wheat crops and to use the straw for thatching. Despite the untimely death of his wife in 1963 at the age of 57, he carried on, but after retirement, returned to live in Milton Ernest in a little cottage overlooking the park where he had spent many happy hours in his younger days watching cricket. 'Living by myself was not my way of life, being one of a large family and a family man myself' (Reg was one of eleven children, and he and his wife had four children).

Since then, Reg has re-married, his present wife having been a neighbour and friend of long-standing. They now live in a stone and thatched cottage in Thurleigh Road, Milton Ernest, similar in many respects to the cottage in which Reg was born. From his cottage home he can see the church to the left, and on the right, on Church Green, the school, both of which he attended in his young days.

EYVOR SIBYL PELHAM REID (NÉE DOYNE-DITMAS)

Eyvor was born in India on 11 February 1908, whilst her father, a Major in the Royal Field Artillery, was serving in India. Her maternal grandfather, Sir Phillip Monoux Payne, farmed at Bourne End near Wootton and Eyvor's parents returned to Wootton after the first World War. Her family have been associated with this part of the county for several centuries. In the chancel of Wootton church there are many monuments to the Monoux family, the oldest being a marble monument to Sir Humphrey Monoux and dated 1680.

HILDA PHOEBE PUDDEPHATT

Hilda was born on 15 December 1891 in Luton, and grew up in Princess Street. Her father was a straw hat manufacturer and owned his own small private factory which was built on one side of the garden. Both of her parents were Lutonians. They had one other child, a boy. Hilda's father died in 1915.

Hilda enjoyed her school days and attended Luton's first Grammar School on Park Square. She went on to teach, her first post being at Buxton Road Church School in 1909. She retired in 1957.

CONSTANCE MARIE ROBINSON (NÉE SAUNDERS)

Connie was born at 21 Bedford Road, Wootton, on Christmas Day in 1909, which is why she was given the name 'Marie'. She was one of eight children, and her parents had a smallholding at their Bedford Road home.

Connie became a teacher, and her first permanent teaching post was a Wootton Primary School, where she herself had once been a pupil.

EVELINE STANTON

Eveline was born on 10 February 1897 in Colmworth village. There were eight children in the family, five boys and three girls. She had more illness than any of the other children, and yet outlived them all.

After a prolonged illness whilst in her teens, Eveline took up poultry farming – her doctor's suggestion. She would have preferred nursing, but felt she hadn't sufficient strength to cope with the demands of nursing.

SIDNEY ERNEST SUMMERLIN

Sid was born on 10 July 1902 in Stagsden, in a thatched cottage which

stood opposite Stagsden church, and was known as the Old Vicarage. There were five children in the family, and his father was a farm worker.

Sid left school and started casual work on the farm until a full-time job came up. Things were very slack at the time. He has continued to work on the farm throughout his working life. Even after retirement at the age of sixty-seven, he worked when the opportunity presented itself. Sid remained a bachelor.

ARTHUR 'LOL' LAWRENCE THEW

'Lol', as he was always known, was born on 31 October 1903 in the end one of three cottages in Harrold High Street, which stood opposite the

present garage. There were three children in the family, and his father worked in the leather trade. His grandfather was a shepherd.

After leaving school at 13, Lol wanted to join the airforce, which he could not do until the age of fifteen. He did get as far as London in an attempt to join up, but failed because of his poor eyesight. He also wanted to go to Australia, but could not because his mother would not consent. He subsequently joined his father in the leather industry.

ERIC THORNE

Eric was born on 9 January 1896 in Woburn and was the third child of five. His father owned a butcher's shop in High Street North, Dunstable, at one time, and was always connected with farming and animals.

In 1921 Eric and his brother Cyril sailed to Australia. It was a very hard life and they had to do odd jobs to earn a living. They slept rough many times, not having sufficient money to pay for lodgings. At one time Eric rode a horse in a race and also entered the boxing ring as a contestant, to make money. Cyril met a girl and settled down, but although Eric was not afraid of hard work, he gave up and came home after two years. A year later he married Maude Durante of Houghton Road and settled down in Markyate where their son Frank was born. In 1930 he bought a piece of land in Beale Street from his father and had a house built, in which he lived until his death in 1985.

JOHN 'JACK' CLIFFORD THORNE

Jack, as he has always been known, was born on 2 April 1907 in Ilford, Essex. His father, a monumental mason, was killed in a road accident involving horses, whilst cycling to work. The fourth child in the family was born shortly after the death of her father, and Jack's mother then returned to live near her parents at Cross End, Thurleigh.

Jack, who regards himself as being self-educated, started work on the farm, and went on to do nursery gardening, and then became a gardening chauffeur, which he describes as the best job he ever had. His employers were wealthy people but very nice people who treated him as a 'human being'. He farmed out of necessity, but points out that farming at that time was poorly paid, and carried low status.

GLADYS LILLIAN WALLIS (NÉE FROST)

Gladys was born on 28 August 1904 in Bassingbourne, Cambridgeshire, which is near Royston. There were seven children in the family, of whom six survived, and her father was a police constable. Gladys's maternal grandfather was a blacksmith by trade, but her grandparents also had a small market garden. They lived in Soham in the Fens, between Ely and Cambridge.

Gladys's parents moved around as her father was posted in different places, but she started school in Bassingbourne and 'loved every minute of it'. She went on to become a teacher herself. She married at twenty-five, and met her husband in the village where she first went to teach. He had just come out of the army when she first knew him and after their marriage, they set up home in Maulden, where she has lived since 1929.

BEATRICE MAY WEBB (NÉE JEFFORD)

May, as she has always been known, was born in Hounslow, Middlesex, on 28 July 1906. Her father was Haynes born, and this is where all of his family lived. At the time May was born, he was working as a builder's labourer – a yardman – in Chiswick, and when he was drafted into the army in 1914, her mother moved back to Haynes to be near his family. May's mother was born in Wiltshire, but had been in service in Hounslow before their marriage.

May's father was killed in action on 4 November 1918, a few days before the armistice was signed.

May's husband's family came from near Biggleswade, where his father was a smallholder. He and his parents moved to May's present cottage home in 1919, and they married in 1933. Her mother-in-law was an independent lady who worked on the land and continued to do so until she was in her seventies, at which time she qualified for a pension. May's husband was a farm worker all his life.

HERBERT WELCH

Herbert was born at Stagsden West End, which is about two miles from Stagsden, in July 1914. He was the youngest of eleven children and his father was a horsekeeper who worked for Mr Howkins at West End Farm.

After working for several years on the farm, Herbert left to work on the railway. He was a ganger for five years, but eventually returned to the farm, and rented a tied cottage near Turvey Grove Farm, which is now a built-up area. Ill-health forced him to retire early, and for the last ten years of his working life he was employed at Bromham Hospital.

HORACE GEORGE WELCH

Horace was born in Stagsden West End on 25 October 1907, in his father's small tied cottage. His father was a horse keeper to a local farmer. There were eleven children in the family, eight of whom were born in this cottage. Horace eventually took over his father's cottage, and four of his own children were born there. His mother died aged eighty-seven, and his father at eighty.

When Horace retired from farming, he applied for a Council house and was eventually housed at Wood End, Kempston.

OLIVER WELLS

Oliver, youngest of nine children, was born at Felmersham Grange, Felmersham, on 10 March 1922. The Wells family are well-known for their business interests, being based in Bedford. Oliver maintains that there was never any pressure on him to join the family business – Charles Wells Ltd. – founded by his grandfather in 1876. Ever since his inaugural flight in a DH Moth at the age of ten, his main ambition was to fly. Having left Uppingham at the age of eighteen, he joined the Royal Air Force and gained great satisfaction from being able to fly. Oliver left the Forces in 1956, shortly before the death of his father. Following his father's death he was obliged to help in the business.

Wing Commander Wells was awarded an OBE in 1992 for services to the community in Bedfordshire.

FREDERICK WALLACE WILDMAN

Fred was born on 27 August 1893 at 1 Cross End, Thurleigh. He was the eldest of seven children and was born in the house in which his grandmother was born and where his parents set up home when they married. Fred's father was a carpenter, wheelwright and undertaker. Fred worked for his father before leaving school, and after leaving school at twelve. In later life he was a very energetic member of his community – in particular within the Church, the Cricket Club, in fund-raising and so on.

Fred lived an active and long life, and enjoyed good health. At the age of ninety-four he was breaking bricks to lay a new driveway!

Index to Locations

Books Published by THE BOOK CASTLE

CHANGES IN OUR LANDSCAPE: ASPECTS OF BEDFORDSHIRE, BUCKINGHAMSHIRE and the CHILTERNS, 1947–1992: from the photographic work of Eric Meadows. 350+ fascinating colour and monochrome pictures by the area's leading landscape photographer. Detailed introduction and captions.

JOURNEYS INTO HERTFORDSHIRE: Anthony Mackay. Foreword by The Marquess of Salisbury, Hatfield House. Nearly 200 superbly detailed ink drawings depict the towns, buildings and landscape of this still predominantly rural county.

JOURNEYS INTO BEDFORDSHIRE: Anthony Mackay. Foreword by The Marquess of Tavistock, Woburn Abbey. A lavish book of over 150 evocative ink drawings.

NORTH CHILTERNS CAMERA, 1863–1954: FROM THE THURSTON COLLECTION IN LUTON MUSEUM: edited by Stephen Bunker. Rural landscapes, town views, studio pictures and unique royal portraits by the area's leading early photographer.

LEAFING THROUGH LITERATURE: WRITERS' LIVES IN HERTFORDSHIRE AND BEDFORDSHIRE: David Carroll. Illustrated short biographies of many famous authors and their connections with these counties.

THROUGH VISITORS' EYES: A BEDFORDSHIRE ANTHOLOGY: edited by Simon Houfe. Impressions of the county by famous visitors over the last four centuries, thematically arranged and illustrated with line drawings.

THE HILL OF THE MARTYR: AN ARCHITECTURAL HISTORY OF ST. ALBANS ABBEY: Eileen Roberts. Scholarly and readable chronological narrative history of Hertfordshire and Bedfordshire's famous cathedral. Fully illustrated with photographs and plans.

LOCAL WALKS: SOUTH BEDFORDSHIRE and NORTH CHILTERNS: Vaughan Basham. Twenty-seven thematic circular walks.

CHILTERN WALKS: HERTFORDSHIRE, BEDFORDSHIRE and NORTH BUCKINGHAMSHIRE: Nick Moon. Completes the trilogy of circular walks, in association with the Chiltern Society.

CHILTERN WALKS: BUCKINGHAMSHIRE: Nick Moon. In association with the Chiltern Society, one of a series of three guides to the whole Chilterns. Thirty circular walks.

CHILTERN WALKS: OXFORDSHIRE and WEST BUCKINGHAMSHIRE: Nick Moon. In association with the Chiltern Society, another book of thirty circular walks.

COUNTRY AIR: SUMMER and AUTUMN: Ron Wilson. The Radio Northampton presenter looks month by month at the countryside's wildlife, customs and lore.

COUNTRY AIR: WINTER and SPRING: Ron Wilson. This companion volume completes the year in the countryside.

BEDFORDSHIRE'S YESTERYEARS: The Family, Childhood and Schooldays: Brenda Fraser-Newstead. Unusual early 20th century reminiscences, with private photographs. Three further themed collections planned.

WHIPSNADE WILD ANIMAL PARK: 'MY AFRICA': Lucy Pendar. Foreword by Andrew Forbes. Introduction by Gerald Durrell. Inside story of sixty years of the Park's animals and people – full of anecdotes, photographs and drawings.

FARM OF MY CHILDHOOD, 1925–1947: Mary Roberts. An almost vanished lifestyle on a remote farm near Flitwick.

SWANS IN MY KITCHEN: The Story of a Swan Sanctuary: Lis Dorer. Foreword by Dr Philip Burton. Tales of her dedication to the survival of these beautiful birds through her sanctuary near Hemel Hempstead.

A LASTING IMPRESSION: Michael Dundrow. An East End boy's wartime experiences as an evacuee on a Chilterns farm at Totternhoe.

EVA'S STORY: CHESHAM SINCE the TURN of the CENTURY: Eva Rance. The ever-changing twentieth-century, especially the early years at her parents' general stores, Tebby's, in the High Street.

DUNSTABLE WITH THE PRIORY, 1100–1550: Vivienne Evans. First volume of three planned on the town's history to the present day.

DUNSTABLE DECADE: THE EIGHTIES: – A Collection of Photographs: Pat Lovering. A souvenir book of nearly 300 pictures of people and events in the 1980s.

DUNSTABLE IN DETAIL: Nigel Benson. A hundred of the town's buildings and features, plus town trail map.

OLD DUNSTABLE: Bill Twaddle. A new edition of this collection of early photographs.

BOURNE AND BRED: A DUNSTABLE BOYHOOD BETWEEN THE WARS: Colin Bourne. An elegantly written, well-illustrated book capturing the spirit of the town over fifty years ago.

ROYAL HOUGHTON: Pat Lovering. Illustrated history of Houghton Regis from the earliest times to the present.

MURDERS and MYSTERIES, PEOPLE and PLOTS: A Buckinghamshire, Bedfordshire and Northamptonshire Miscellany: John Houghton. This fascinating book of true tales roams around three counties and covers three centuries.

LEGACIES: Tales of Luton and the North Chilterns: Vic Lea. 25 Mysteries and stories based on fact, including Luton Town Football Club. Many photographs.

ECHOES: TALES and LEGENDS of BEDFORDHSIRE and HERTFORDSHIRE: Vic Lea. Thirty, compulsively retold historical incidents.

THE CHANGING FACE OF LUTON: An Illustrated History: Stephen Bunker, Robin Holgate and Marian Nichols. Luton's development from earliest times to the present busy industrial town. Illustrated in colour and monochrome. The three authors from Luton Museum are all experts in local history, archaeology, crafts and social history.

BETWEEN THE HILLS: The Story of Lilley, a Chiltern Village: Roy Pinnock. A priceless piece of our heritage – the rural beauty remains but the customs and way of life described here have largely disappeared.

THE MEN WHO WORE STRAW HELMETS: POLICING LUTON, 1840–1974: Tom Madigan. Meticulously chronicled history; dozens of rare photographs; author served Luton Police for nearly fifty years.

THE TALL HITCHIN SERGEANT: A Victorian Crime Novel based on fact: Edgar Newman. Mixes real police officers and authentic background with an exciting storyline.

Specially for Children

ADVENTURE ON THE KNOLLS: A STORY OF IRON AGE BRITAIN: Michael Dundrow. Excitement on Totternhoe Knolls as ten-year-old John finds himself back in those dangerous times, confronting Julius Caesar and his army.

THE RAVENS: ONE BOY AGAINST THE MIGHT OF ROME: James Dyer. On the Barton hills and in the south-east of England as the men of the great fort of Ravensburgh (near Hexton) confront the invaders.

Further titles are in preparation.
All the above are available via any bookshop, or from the publisher and bookseller

THE BOOK CASTLE
**12 Church Street, Dunstable, Bedfordshire, LU5 4RU
Tel: (0582) 605670**